# WRITERS

# ON

# WRITERS

Published in partnership with

WRITERS
SEAN
O'BEIRNE
ON
HELEN
GARNER
WRITERS

Black Inc.

Published by Black Inc.
in association with the University of Melbourne and State Library Victoria.

Black Inc.,
an imprint of Schwartz Books Pty Ltd
Level 1, 221 Drummond Street, Carlton Victoria 3053, Australia
enquiries@blackincbooks.com
www.blackincbooks.com

State Library Victoria
328 Swanston Street
Melbourne Victoria 3000 Australia
www.slv.vic.gov.au

The University of Melbourne
Parkville Victoria 3010 Australia
www.unimelb.edu.au

9781760642785 (hardback)
9781743821992 (ebook)

A catalogue record for this
book is available from the
National Library of Australia

Cover design by Peter Long, Akiko Chan and Tristan Main
Typesetting by Tristan Main, Aira Pimping and Marilyn de Castro
Photograph of Helen Garner: Darren James
Photograph of Sean O'Beirne: Paul Hermes

Printed in China by 1010 Printing

*To G., R. and T.*

What I love, what I need, first in Helen Garner's writing is a particular kind of *closeness to self* – the good, greedy, mistaken, emotional, fierce, sceptical, changing and disrupting *self*. There is, always, Garner's sheer skill at observation, with sentences, with words in combination: but a writer can have that and you still don't attach, in some way: once a certain level of skill has been cleared, the real affinity is to the emotion-news, the thing about life, about people, that the writer tells you it's alright to think. And her fierceness for more self got me, very young. The way that if her more individual self feels something she *says* it – and then finds out what the consequences are. And not, as most of us do, hide that more individual feeling, maybe say it to someone later, after the meeting, at the pub, when we get home. Or say it right away, but

1

only in a language that's also always sending out the message: don't be threatened by me, I'm with the group, I promise. I'm saying 'engaged' and 'impactful' and 'engaged' again. I'm going to stick to what we've already agreed can be said, and use the words we've already agreed to say it. And so much of our working life – our *life* – gets made from a series of safe generalities.

Garner's faith is that, at least sometimes, you should try for something less group-safe, less group-controlled. And it all depends on this concentration on the near-to-me: on what seems more individual, close enough to the mind and body's first apprehension, close to what can be reliably experienced by a self and its senses, before some more abstract intellectual or institutional system starts to try to do its over-organising, its smoothing, its taking too-far-away. Starts to say: let's not talk about that. Or: we don't talk about that. In her fiction and non-fiction, Helen Garner says: *I'll* talk about that. I'll give you exactly what people hide all the time, my not-as-socially-approved *awareness*. I'll tell you what seems to come straight from just these good and bad amounts of *self* before it all gets nicely socialised away. So, in *Monkey Grip*: I'll tell you what it was really like – the sex, the love – with him, I'll tell how I wanted him and when he was so bad and incompetent I wanted him more. Or in *The First Stone*: I'll tell you what I really felt when some group wanted to punish an individual too much, because They had decided there'd be some new rules. Over and over, in different ways in different places in her work, she says: let it live, let the more individual self survive.

In an essay just called 'I', Garner wrote that once she saw:

> a row of tall trees across the tops of which a creeper had grown so hungrily and aggressively that it had formed a thick, strangling mat: the trees were no longer individuals, but had become part of a common mass. I found

> this spectacle strangely repellent. It filled me
> with horror.

I feel this too, a lot. I grew up with people who were different from me and who more or less demanded I be like them. People who wouldn't let me find what I had to have to feed and balance and maintain my own separate-enough little self. Reacting and overreacting to that, I developed a pretty exaggerated sense of *I'll never be in some clump of Them*. And so I'm always ready to hear someone say: keep as much individual self as you can. It will do good. It will always help you see what They do wrong.

But I love Garner's writing because she *also* shows that trying for a more individual self can be as stupid, bad, even evil, as trying to force anybody into some group. Garner's extraordinary literary intelligence comes from this: she's never just contrarian for the individual, she shows that trying for more individual-ness has its own bad compounding momentum, its own conformity for itself. Its own habits, traps. And failure, and sadness. That, for example, having made what you thought was a necessarily more separate self, you could then find to your surprise – out there – mostly how desperately you need other people. You can try to live, as Garner says in one story, by holding onto your own 'hard rail of will'. But, she says much more often, a self is made only with the help of other human beings. By testing yourself against them, being cared for by them. In that same 'I' essay, after confessing the 'horror' of others, she says, '[T]he older I get, and paradoxically the more *hermit-like* I become in the wake of my spectacular failures to be a wife, the more I am obliged by experience to recognise the interdependence of people.' To see that we do 'form each other'. Garner's work shows how you might have to make a huge effort to save enough of a self – against family, against authority (whatever seems *against* you) – and then have to make the maybe even more difficult effort to come back to enough others. To find enough of a law, a rule, a family, a home. The 'horror' turns out to be of too little sense of individual self *and* too much. Garner's writing is full of people caught, locked, in extremes of feeling they have too little self or too much: from Nicola, in *The Spare Room*, who smiles all the time, lies all the time, because 'all my life I've never wanted to bore people with the way I feel'; to Philip in *The Children's Bach*, living so free, so unconnected, enjoying so much casual sex, and thinking sometimes he might put a razor to his throat; all the way to the wretched Robbie Farquharson, in *This House of Grief*, who, the night he drowned his three children, asked the police, 'What's the likely scenario, for me? … I mean, what sort of thing's going to happen to *me*, now?'

Throughout her writing life, Garner has fought to see both these needs – for me, for others – which so often contradict, which never go away. She's been able to hold, order and present this permanent human conflict which we so often try to replace with our clumsy, insistent, angry demands that there could be just *more me!* or *more group!* – Garner calls all of that 'clonking' certainty. And she says: it has to be both, always both, you have to make the effort to see and respect and allow for both needs. The conflict between *me* and *them*, no matter how much we want it to be, is never easily *solvable*.

But that leads me on to my own confusion about why I need Garner's writing, and my own wish that some conflicting needs could just be solved away. Because I'm like her and not like her, and I wish I *was* more like her, and I *don't* wish that (I don't?) and – off we go to the Land of Many Writing Confusions. When I write, in my smaller way, I do want to show the same problem as Garner. I try to show that a more separate individual sensibility is good and necessary, a way to fight Them, and also always in danger of becoming stupid or sour or vicious. But here's the difference:

Garner worked and worked to show the dilemma of individual and group *openly as herself*. She found a way to be unusually honest about the problem of how to regulate a self – all the awkward, embarrassing *details* of this – in her own name, using her own memories, own feelings, own thoughts. To say less socially acceptable things identifiably as Helen Garner. I use the opposite method: I'll say less socially acceptable things *only if I'm pretending to be other people*. It sounds ridiculous when I say it as baldly as that, but it is of course the more common method. The writer (or actor or comedian) says what usually can't be said 'in character'. That way it stays just a little, just enough, hypothetical. You get to conduct a sort of test with a pretend person: here's something *as if* someone actually said it. This gives you needed protection against Them. I often think of that line from Auden, in his poem about Edward Lear: 'They / Were so many and big like dogs'. I think They *are* so many, I think They *are* big like dogs. I think if you say something even mildly unorthodox, the They of this world can come and get you and hurt you so bad. I think people's aggression and egotism and fear of change will make them ruin another person's life, for saying something a bit different, easily. Happens all the time. And I want protection from *my* self, as well, from what my aggression and egotism and fear will make if I come out with too much, too soon: shame, defensiveness, paranoia: all the nasty psychical products that come from a feeling of the loss of the usual controls.

Saying things as someone else isn't just scaredly protective, though; it's also freeing, interesting, fun. Your usual controls can all be set too high: pretend to be someone else and you'll find unexpected thought and emotion are released in this *as if* experiment. You can let out what could be thought of as the good aggression, very refreshing but not vicious, not bigoted, amounts of *fuck no* and *fuck that*, as well as quieter not usually permitted emotions: remorse, or grief. It all becomes more available when you don't have to stick to only your usual, your habitual, repertoire. I've sometimes been so happy in it, the pretending-to-be-other-people method. I've said things I never knew I could say. And not been mauled by the others or myself because I did.

But then there's Garner, who takes the risk to work out in the open, with so much less fiction protection. Her writing makes an argument that you don't need that protection, should maybe come out and fight as yourself. I find that argument puts a special pressure on me now, because, I think, of an unease I feel about pretending to be other people, so much, so often. Of using any method too exclusively to save or free me; letting it become a habit, the thing I do, not something I'm really weighing the costs of. I don't want to start turning against the impersonation method too quickly. It *is* freeing. It *is* necessary. Look at the size and beauty and wisdom of what has been made using that method: everything from *Hamlet* to *Middlemarch* to *Portnoy's Complaint*. We *have* to talk as others. It is, often, the only way to tell enough of what we are. And yet, having done some of it, in my junior way, I already feel the need for an antidote. Or at least to look hard at the other method, the good work of less impersonation. Look hard at Garner, one of its best practitioners. Try to see what she gains, what she risks, from doing it on her side. And try a little of that side myself. Without going too far and thinking I can suddenly transfer over – that would be its own kind of wishful stupidity about how much anyone can 'change', and a severe underestimation of how difficult it would be to confess as much, as skilfully, as yourself, as Helen Garner does. But I can try some. A starting amount of more open confession. And with any luck, as I try this, you'll get the chance to think about what you need, what methods you've used to save or protect yourself. How much you think should be told, just as you, and how much shouldn't be. Or to put it another way: what you believe human beings can and can't do together, very openly, and honestly.

An interviewer once asked Garner: 'You talked about how people have one story in them, which they tell repeatedly in various versions … what is that story for you?'

And Garner replied: 'I suppose it would have to be the story of me fighting with my father, and of course, by extension, fighting all the others who represent the father figure to me, like big institutions, powerful men, expert knowledge and theory and all those sorts of things.'

One of the places you can best see what the father, what authority, is to Garner, and the way she had to make her self against it, is in her story 'Postcards from Surfers'. You feel the weight of him, his presence, as a heavy continuous amount of: don't you be different, we've already decided this, why would you wanna do that, and I don't *think* so. 'Look at those idiots,' he says, because a couple of people are surfing. He watches the footy on TV with 'bursts of contemptuous laughter'. 'Don't tramp sand everywhere,' he says. And, 'Going to help Mum with the dishes, are you, miss?' Even his smaller actions have a kind of complacent physical selfishness: when he makes a sandwich and a piece of meat flaps loose, he 'rounds it up with a large, dramatic scooping movement and a sympathetic grimace of the lower lip'. As he chews, 'he breathes heavily through his nose', and 'the noise of his eating fills the room'. The thing to try to hold onto here is what it would've been like to grow up with this as your *world*. To be a little kid, and to grow up where the most important authority nearby, your own father, was making everything into: I will say what there is and there is nothin' else. 'My father,' Garner wrote in her *Diaries*, 'is incapable of conversation. His speech is almost rhetorical: he speaks very slowly with the emphasis of someone giving important information to a listener whose understanding he has no faith in.' In that shrewd book *The Presentation of Self in Everyday Life*, Erving Goffman wrote that even though we can't just tell the truth when we're together, can't say all of 'what actually exists' (it's just too dangerous, would cause too much conflict), we can at least work together to make an agreed substitute, something we can all bear to have as enough reality, for now. Goffman calls this 'the working consensus' and says most of our social life is made of it. What people like Garner's father are trying for is a kind of extra demand that there won't even be a 'working consensus', they'll do it *all*. Even that second, weaker 'nice' sort of meaning-making, they'll make all of that as well.

And I know that world: one of the strongest affinities I have with Garner is that she'll show me this so well, remind me of it, take me back to it and make me try to figure out what it was, what it did; this over-determined, over-regulated world; a world, a home, where you don't even get to make a nice ordinary hypocrisy together, but where one bloke decides what the story's gonna be, over and over and over. I know the boredom and resentment that comes from having to live in that. Watching him display himself, his limited amount, again and again, and demand that it be yours as well. I grew up in the outer suburbs with that pretty heavy *load of bloke* over me, being told anything new is idiotic, and there really were only maybe four things to do, only four choices of activity (footy/ cricket, eat stuff, watch TV, 'go for a walk'). And even when I got further away from the house, there didn't seem to be very much more that was possible. This was in the bleaker, more concreted and tan-barked Australian outer suburbs, in the mid-1980s, in what was culturally a much more bloke-homogenous, sport-homogenous *situation* in our country. What it all gave me was the feeling, not the reality exactly – it's not like anyone imprisoned me, exactly – but the feeling of being surrounded every day by nothing but a bunch of blokes goin': we're all doin' this, we're all playin' cricket, we're all kickin' the footy, you should do that, you should do that, you should do that. Why wouldn't you wanna do that?

But even as a kid you know that there's something wrong with what you'll make out of all this – you can sense, and are ashamed of and confused by, what are, or what *might be*, your over-reactions. I knew my parents loved me, I knew they didn't mean to hurt me, really. I knew even as a little kid that there was something wrong in reacting as if it was an assault to go to Jells Park for another family BBQ. That it was not an intended assault, it was a kindly assault, a sort of 'I never meant to hurt the boy's feelings, Jesus, I thought it might be nice if he went outside for five fuckin minutes, boy'll go blind if he fuckin stays in here reading all day' kind of assault. The guilt comes because everybody has a right to ask: why don't you want what we want? Don't you like us? *They* can fairly ask that. You hurt them, too. Although there was plenty of evidence around of what our majority *They*/grouse-blokes-and-fellas group would do to you if you were carrying around even just a bit more difference than I was. There was a chubby round-faced boy in my street who was called 'Gavin the Punce'. Or: 'The Punce'. There he goes, 'The Punce'. That was his *childhood*. And he had a sister who was older and bigger and heavy-set, she was always called 'Gavin's brother'. Fun, eh? So I watched myself. I laid low. I was in *some* trouble, a not-quite-quantifiable amount of trouble; and I couldn't judge how much to make, or not make, from there. Make with? Make against? The problem of the self can't be reduced beneath a certain point: you will be stuck managing a consciousness that always seems so stubbornly local to your one brain and body. But the comedy and pathos of being a kid is that you don't know this. The problem of you is both enormous and something you think you maybe shouldn't have at all. You think to yourself: it's not like bigger things in the world, it's not like politics or anything.

And the shame and confusion is that to you it is like a politics, is just like a politics, as big as a politics (so stupid to feel this, so shameful), to you it's the fight over the government of you, the continuous fight over this ridiculous, tiny but to *you* very valuable territory.

Now imagine bringing all that to *Monkey Grip*. I read it when I was seventeen. What got me, what still gets me, is the concentrated amount of self that's in it. *Monkey Grip* is saturated in one consciousness, and seeing this, page after page, was one of the first big confirmations that things could be like this, that this was what had already happened to me (or I'd done it) and that it was contradictorily interesting and delicious and bad and lonely to be so steeped in, waterlogged with, the problem of *me*.

In *Monkey Grip*, everything is narrowed down to Nora. The only things that get into the book are things that are presented most directly and immediately to her senses; what she most directly and immediately feels, sees, hears. There's almost no history in *Monkey Grip*, no 'context'. Nora does say that she lives in an old brown house, a mile from the middle of the city. And as the book goes on we're also told that she has a little daughter called Grace, and that Nora and Grace live poor, with musicians and actors, in one shabby share house after another. But that's about it. After that, people and places mostly just – appear. Nora will say: Clive came over. Cobby's back. I saw Martin. I saw Jessie, Javo, Lou, Selina, Willy, Rita, Ange. I went to the Tower. I went with Bill to Shakahari. It's a little disconcerting, at first, but soon you get the idea; you're so close in to Nora she's not going to stop and more formally explain, 'Willy moved from Adelaide two years ago where his parents were both teachers, his mother, primary, and the father at a technical college.' No, no: the voluptuousness in this writing, this method, is that there's no need for any of that. She's talking to you *as if you already knew*. It's as if you're already part of her consciousness, and so many things never even have to be explained.

And so close *in* to this particular kind of individual consciousness, there are no bigger outside events, can't be any bigger outside events. At one point Nora says it's election day, 'and Labor was going to get done like a dinner'. *Monkey Grip* was published in 1977, and, you could guess, was mostly written in the two or three years before that. So this must be the election of 1975 – the election Labor lost after the Dismissal. And the Dismissal, it's fair to say, was one of the biggest events that ever happened in Australia. But not here. Not in this book, which in its good stubborn exclusiveness is saying everyone can already talk about the Dismissal. Everyone *already* knows how to do that. Leave it out, leave everything like that out, leave out every bigger or more general or more instrumental kind of ordering information, any kind of bigger arguments or argument-structures, and then you'll restore something, make a claim for something. The unofficial part. The inside half of us. The everything else we are. That part of the human that is least able to be turned into, or helped by, bigger kinds of shared thinking, intellection, concepts. You'll really see this strange thing in us: our more primary animal and psychological need. *Monkey Grip*, more than anything else, is a record of this: the less social kind of need that lies inside a self, the more basic need that can *grip* you, and that is so hard to stop, to reason yourself out of.

Nora needs Javo. He's one of the people who's at the brown house on the corner, or at the Tower, with Willy and Ange and Lou and everybody. But it's also soon obvious that he's in worse trouble than any of the others, he's wilder, takes more drugs (heroin, speed), is more vulnerable, and more beautiful because he's more vulnerable. Javo is beautiful in a wrecked way; tall, slim, black-haired, blue-eyed, but also often untidy, dirty, scabby; he's like Lord Byron and Peter Pan: a mad, bad and dangerous Boy Who Wouldn't Grow Up.

A meaner way to say it would be: *because* he's so good-looking he's looked after, never has to learn; he's the least socially competent of all of them, more of a boy, full of a boy's purposeless energy: always crashing down stairs or wrenching doors open, and with a boy's earnestness: 'toiling' to write a letter, in his 'painstaking printing'. Nora says his life is a 'messy holiday of living off his friends'.

But then Nora finds – and there's a terrible psychical logic to this – an exaggerated amount of *me* becoming an exaggerated amount of *for one other*. She starts making *as much* consciousness about a self, but now only *for Javo*. It's a mistaken way out of too much self, a mistake you make because you have no skill at reducing the sense of self, at getting by with less of the thing altogether. With no sure models from the family, no good examples of how to get the proportions right there, you're all set up to keep your first exaggerated amount and then try for a crude kind of transfer. And Nora confusedly knows that this is what's happening, she says several times: people like me are always 'given' it all away'. Or that all she's done, in this love, is 'leaked myself away towards you'. But as often she doesn't understand, can't understand and keeps asking herself, *why*, why so much for him, why Javo, Javo, Javo? And then doing more of it: where is Javo, is Javo coming over? Gracie says, 'If it's Javo I know! You're going to cry of happiness!' He appears to her as this huge beautiful substituting *someone else* she needs so badly: over and over she says she sees his blue eyes, his fierce blue eyes, his wrecked blue eyes, his blue eyes in his lantern head, over and over, his blue eyes and his bony body, over and over 'struck dumb, by the beauty of his colours'. And very early on, when she's beginning to find out what the rest of him is like, and people are starting to tell her she shouldn't be with him, he's no good, he's a junkie, stop it, she says: 'I can't. I won't. I thought of his skin and the way I could sense his skull and his crazy eyes.'

By this point they've already fucked. And what's so affecting and sad in it all is that they do sometimes get the thing they want most, which is to get out of the over-concentrated selves they've made. When they fuck, he can call off his self-absorption, and go to her properly, really be with her, give to her without trying for too much for himself. And she can do that too. In the fucking – in that care, that pleasure – both of them find their too-much falls away, and they become the best and kindest selves they can be:

> … the way it happened was, that we began to stroke each other, and to kiss, and after a long, long time of slow, gentle touching and pausing, and kissing like an idle game that turned serious (he held my head hard with his two hands, we kissed and kissed) I rolled on to him and we fucked ever so gently. 'Wait, oh wait,' he whispered, and I waited, and he started again with the

slow and steady rolling under me, his mad crooked face very sweet in front of my eyes; I felt the thin bones in his shoulders, and my heart dissolved to see him change away from abruptness to this kindness.

And:

Nobody knows what I get out of Javo, or out of knowing him. I don't know to explain. It's that when we fuck, or can be together quietly sometimes, *we touch each other*. No-one else gets that close to me. He behaves towards me, then, with tenderness, holds me when I'm half asleep, he says my name and looks into my face.

But Nora finds out slowly that this kindness and tenderness can't last, can't survive, because it doesn't have enough to do with everyday life, everyday jobs, all the more boring things that really test if you can be together. They go on holiday to the beach, in Tasmania: he won't plan properly, he won't pack anything ('Oh shit,' he croaks, 'we don't need mosquito coils, all that shit'), she has to do everything, and when they finally get to the beach he plunges on ahead in his stolen thongs, not even talking to her. Then at the campsite, he suddenly turns to her, his arms stretched out like a child's: 'Nor, help me – I'm freaking out.' This kind of stuff happens for months. Exquisite pleasure, exquisite kindness, their best, best selves, then he doesn't turn up, he forgets he's supposed to, she worries, she lends him money, waits for him, lends him more money. Their whole relationship starts to look like a cruel kind of trap – a trying to be with someone else that's only really an addiction. With her addiction less grossly obvious than his, but as strong, really. Nora says – and she can *say* this – 'Smack habit, love habit – what's the difference?' But if there's one thing the book shows it's that it can be so hard to give up on the hope that you could stay in that other place, where your self seems to be *un*-selfed enough; reduced, calmed, healed. Next to that, the promise of that, the everyday doesn't matter, for a while.

What's extraordinary is that *Monkey Grip* can hold so much of what could be repetitive or unpleasant (Ugh, Javo, *again*) and make it bearable. It does this partly by taking all this anguished private telling and cooling it with just enough of what is outside the self: not, again, with information from the very biggest structures – politics, social theories – there's none of that, but instead the sense of being kept only in one self is relieved by carefully chosen exterior physical detail. 'Atomic' bright concrete at the public baths, the 'flutter' of poplars over 'an ancient grey picket fence'. When Nora and Javo are still on holiday in Tasmania, they stay at a motel: and there is his ignoring her and falling asleep, but there are also the clean sheets, the hiss of the waves, the moon on their skin. Nora's self-problems are always placed between pictures of what she can see, what her senses can apprehend, but what is *not* her: in with her close consciousness, we're also given a sky, 'covered with a fine net of almost invisible cloud', or kids asleep, 'cast across the bed in attitudes of struggle and flight'. It's so, so skilfully done.

But then there is something odder, more controversial, in the method of *Monkey Grip*, which is that all the information that I, and maybe you, so badly need about what a self does, how it tries to love, was taken unusually directly from actual people, people Garner knew. Her actual boyfriend, her actual friends. Shaped, yes, so skilfully selected, and cooled, but still: much more directly taken. In that 'I' essay, Garner said:

> Shouldn't a *real* writer be writing about something other than herself and her immediate circle? I've been haunted by this question since 1977 when a reviewer of *Monkey Grip* asked irritably what the fuss was about: as far

as he could see, all I'd done was publish my diaries. I went round for years after that in a lather of defensiveness: 'It's a *novel*, thank you very much'. But I'm too old to bother with that crap any more. I might as well come clean. I *did* publish my diary. That's exactly what I did. I left out what I thought were the boring bits, wrote bridging passages, and changed all the names.

And so the Javo in the book really was the same as the boy she knew, saying all those things, doing all those things. And people often don't like this. The man who was Javo didn't like it. In 'I' Garner quotes him as saying that for a long time he thought *Monkey Grip* was the 'worst thing that ever happened' to him. And years later in a documentary on the book, he said, 'I hated it … I'm painted as this self-destructive fool, really … I mean what *Monkey Grip* does, it … gives Helen quite a bit of dignity … doesn't give me much.'

And this is something else those fiction protections are for: they protect you from others, but they also properly *protect the others*. Protect the other people you have to take so many bits and pieces off, in order to tell what you need to tell. The usual fiction protection rule is: don't take so much from any one person. It hurts too much, it's too much of a breaking of the necessary, the good part of the social 'consensus' that nobody has to abruptly get shown a bunch of truth about themselves. We all see more, from the outside, of what each other is, but we can't bear it said or suddenly displayed, printed, published, because we all have to keep going with what we've managed to assemble so far. People will be very hurt if you show too much of a vulnerable, trying self, all at once. This is another important reason so much of the vulnerability and unsuccess of the human personality is often only shown in literature (or movies, or comedy), which conceals the real source of the information. You mix the details of whoever

'Javo' was with the details of whoever 'Lou' was – or 'Martin', or 'Bill' – a little of each. And this way, mixing it up enough, everybody's protected more. And you, the fiction writer, you still get what you wanted. Right? Good?

And so then the question comes: why do it the way Garner does it, in *Monkey Grip*? And again, in another fiction, *The Spare Room*? Garner has said that she pretty much took all the incidents and details in *The Spare Room* from one friend, who is put into the book as 'Nicola', poor deluded Nicola who has stage-four cancer but thinks vitamin C and ozone treatments can 'scoop' that cancer right out of her body. You could think: maybe don't take so exclusively from her? Given that she was even more vulnerable than most people trying to work a self? The more specific way of putting the question would be: what do you get, taking so much from this actual person, that *can't be got* with the safer method of mixing up the people? Karl Ove Knausgaard asks exactly this in his book

*My Struggle*, which is six volumes – more than *3500 pages* – of taking and showing, publishing to the whole world, what happens to actual him and actual everyone around him; his own anxiety, selfishness, embarrassing sexual greediness, embarrassing sexual incompetence (that he won't let himself masturbate until he is nineteen, and then later when he does get to have sex he prematurely ejaculates, a lot), as well as his father's alcoholism, his wife's anxiety and self-saving laziness, her blindness to the fact that he does almost all of the housework and looking after the children, all this, all this, he tells and tells and tells. And he says, in answer to the question why, that the social agreement we make to not directly tell about these things *has* to be broken. As harsh and 'inhuman' as it sounds, it *has* to be broken to help and to free people. Because if you don't do it, whole lives (his life, his wife's life) are more often lost to the social agreement, more often distorted or spoiled by how much *isn't said*.

Which might sound fanciful, until you think how people can go on not saying *the* most important thing they privately know about their marriage, or a friend, or their work, for years. How people can live in an unhappy continuous dishonesty, for years. Decades.

I think with Garner there is this sense of having to break or blast open an existing social agreement because sometimes you *have* to force more truth into it. That you have to show people what they've become too distortedly social to see. This is certainly true of Nicola, who's made so much for the 'consensus' that she can't take care of herself or the people around her, who is very physically ill, and will die soon, but whenever some serious new problem is explained to her, just 'beams a smile', 'a frightful, agonised, social smile'. And is told by the 'Helen' in *The Spare Room*: 'I can't stand the falseness … You've got to get ready.' And Nicola, weeping, is finally able to confess what she hasn't said enough of: 'You see, all my life I've never wanted to bore people with the way I feel.'

But Garner also has a sweeter sense of this unusual truth-telling, a faith that the less social truth doesn't have to be a terrible news: it can be a liberation, a joyful thing. She shows that in one of the first pieces she ever published, 'Why Does the Women Get All the Pain?', an essay about how, when she was a teacher, she went ahead and told her class of thirteen-year-olds an unusually honest amount about sex. The kids found drawings of dicks had been made in their books on Ancient Greek history and culture, and were all giggling about it ('It's in my book too!'). And Garner said, Look, do you want to talk about this? She liked the kids. She trusted them. And she paid them the deep compliment of saying: I really will tell you anything you ask. And they *asked*. They wrote it all on pieces of paper:

HOW ARE SPURM PRODUCED?

WHY CAN'T A LADY HAVE A BABY
WHEN SHE'S OLD?

WHAT'S A FRANGER?

CAN YOU FUCK EVERY DAY?

WHY DOES THE WOMEN GET ALL
THE PAIN?

And Garner told them. In plain words, too. She said: 'the words some people think of as dirty words are the best words, the right words, to use when you are talking about sex. So I'm not going to say, "sexual intercourse", I'm going to say "fuck" and I'm going to say "cock".' And through this extra telling, the what you're not supposed to say, she and the kids found something better; they saw each other:

Lou in the front row fixes his beautiful serious eyes on me and says, 'Miss, what does a cunt look like?' I tell them, like a flower, and girls should get a mirror and look at themselves. Everyone laughs at this, but it's for pleasure and joy. The boys turn to glance at the girls, and their faces look both curious and tender.

There's a strikingly similar passage in another essay, 'A Scrapbook, an Album', when Garner and her sisters tell more, give more: 'I'm scared of you,' Garner tells one of them. And the sister says back, 'I'm scared of you, too.' And they 'laugh, and look away'. But then they turn back and look at each other 'curiously. Gently.'

And me, smaller writer me, I do see the possibility of this, the beauty of it, the goodness. But I also have a kind of starting stupidity about it, some wall or blank. It's the difference I talked about before, between a near fundamental faith in good-openness, and a near fundamental faith in good-concealment. The difference between finding out you need to confess *as you*, and finding out you can make your confession only if you pretend to be other people.

Garner, in *Monkey Grip*, very beautifully gives me the most private things, takes me to the most private, least defended ways you can be:

> What was it about him? Whenever he touched my cunt, my clitoris seemed to be in the exact spot where he first came in contact with my flesh.

And gives me the gift of not really hiding who this actually happened to. That it's not in a more disguised fiction *does* make it especially valuable to me. Partly because I do believe that the social agreement should be more strongly broken, sometimes, for the reason Garner and crazy, desperate Knausgaard say. We'll just keep living in too many lies, too much 'consensus' if we don't do some extra breaking of the usual protections – and even of the usual *fiction* protections. Even literary fiction doesn't break through enough sometimes: we need the extra strength of that more separate, more individual self *not* pretending to be other people, *not* doing impersonations, appearing as itself, using its real name, where it really lives, with the people who are really around it. We need what people now call 'auto-fiction': a form that's still fiction, still has all the selection and arrangement of fiction, but with pieces of the actual placed in among the necessary subterfuge. A form still with the necessary *as if,* but also carrying a special delivery of *it was.*

But then, how much do *I* have to do this? In his book *The Anxiety of Influence,* Harold Bloom says that some writers put a special pressure on other writers because they're so good at pretending to be other people, have so much 'freedom of representation'. I think Garner puts a special pressure on other writers because she's so free *from* representation. Doesn't need a lot of it. Can tell you about her own clit, less representation necessary.

And representing, impersonating, starts to seem like a failure to be real, as honest as you could be, if you were braver, didn't need to hide. When I read something like Garner's *radical honesty from one self*, I know it's so valuable, but I feel like a student who has the sum demonstrated but will never understand how to do it. I read with something like respect *and* confusion Montaigne saying: 'I am loath even to have thoughts which I cannot publish'. Or, more particularly, Knausgaard saying that he didn't masturbate until he was nineteen, and then telling, as no-one but himself, how he did manage to get that job done. Or Sheila Heti, in *Motherhood*, saying: my partner Miles wanted to put his cock in my ass, and we fucked like that for a while, but then I realised I didn't want him to come in there, so he pulled out and came outside me, like he always does. And you think: at book events now – 'Sheila Heti at Toronto Library' – everyone knows that. It's *so* private. But it *can* be said. And that does remind me of an even stronger amount, thrown down by Maggie Nelson, at the very start of *The Argonauts*:

> Instead the words *I love you* come tumbling out of my mouth in an incantation the first time you fuck me in the ass, my face smashed against the cement floor of your dank and charming bachelor pad. You had *Molloy* by your bedside and a stack of cocks in a shadowy unused shower stall. Does it get any better? *What's your pleasure?* you asked, then stuck around for an answer.

Oh! The defiance of it! She's saying: I am this, this is my life, and I *don't* have to hide it. As Garner, Knausgaard, Heti are all insisting: I will not hide. And it's often about sex, of course, something to do with sex that is given, revealed, because – despite nearly twenty-five years of internet porn, despite all the attempts to make sex the same as any other entertainment – sex is still where we are the least official, least 'proper', least defended. Naked, and making those faces, having to show less socially, more riskily, more vulnerably that we really want something, or to give it.

Here's how, and how much, I've been able to tell about sex, so far. I wrote a story called 'Mands '88'. It was about having sex for the first time, and being so awe-struck by it, at really doing this fabled thing at last. And also about not knowing how to do it, being quite awkward and finding out things I did not know. I put in some lines about being so shocked the vagina has wetness in it, because I believed it would be soft and velvety inside, like a lovely glove? And all this was made pretty closely from my memories of what really happened to me, out in the outer suburbs, in my little bedroom, on my little 'trundle' bed, in 1988. But I didn't, *couldn't*, tell it as just myself. I made up another boy – and this is so strange but also so comforting to me – I told it *as* one of the blokes who so oppressed me when I was in the outer suburbs, I told it as one of those fellas around me goin', 'This kid doesn't even know who won the Brownlow!' I told my private sex story, something I am afraid of or embarrassed by, by pretending to be him. I mixed my memories, my self, with what I imagined to be his voice, his self. It slowly made me less ashamed of myself, and like him a lot better. He helped me say something, and I got to realise I'm closer to him than I'd suspected, that all this could have happened to *him*. He could be this nervous. He could love, and be afraid he's not going to be loved, as much as me. Which is sure something I didn't think about him when I was at high school. I might have started out hating the guy and wanting to mock him, needing to get all the aggression that comes from difference out, and I *can* still do some of that; but the more I mix my self with his, an awareness of possible sameness starts to flow in. It's an old, old idea about what making fiction does, but I have found it to be true. George Eliot called it 'the extension of sympathies'. Arundhati Roy's phrase for it is 'softening the borders'. It's so nice, such an unexpected victory to be able to dissolve my usual resentment, and make amounts of him and me say:

Mands and me, we did that thing for so long where you keep your jeans on but you try and root. With your jeans on … it's really frustrating. It feels nice. It's really frustrating.

And:

The first time we had sex all the way I didn't even come. I was so – I don't know, whatever I was – that I didn't even remember that you did, that that was what you did when you finished. I think I was so shocked to finally have my cock in there and like really be doing it I just moved for twenty minutes and then

I just *stopped*. But then later we were doing it again and I had this incredible like electric feeling all up and then really at the tip of my cock, *so* much more than when you do yourself, like by yourself, the whole feeling was so incredible and I pulled out and looked down and saw at the end of the condom there was this white blob there. And out loud I just went – not even to her, or myself, I don't know who – I just went – 'oh my God!'

The problem is that the impersonation-mixing method is good for opening up the psyche, seeing and admitting your many-facedness, but not so useful when you need to experience yourself more as *one*. When you need to make an argument, to take a stand. Be *less* changeable. Not be, for the moment, so interested in 'softening' to Them. Not interested in saying things also partly as someone else. There are, after all, a lot of things in life you can't say 'in character'. I've been in love with how much I *can* say in character, and the danger of course is I'll just get lost in the impersonations and never say enough as myself. That too is an old, old idea of what fiction can do to you, and I have found that danger to be every bit as real as the lovely benefits. I am often not direct enough in arguments. I won't say explicitly what sometimes should be said bluntly to strangers, or someone I love – to any other person. I can be confrontational if I'm putting on a voice, a persona. This works especially with rude people, or milder kinds of everyday narcissists, people bubbled in their own self, people who won't recognise me properly, won't give me a chance to be their equal. I can get too easily defeated by that, it reminds me, I think, of *him* (it is what Garner, in her *Diaries*, calls 'Dad territory'). I pretended to be French once, all day, when I had a job selling snacks and coffee at a corporate convention. As corporate big boys flicked their credit cards at me I was *very* French back to them: 'You do it. On the masshine. You tap the *caird.*' But this pretending in difficult or boring interactions, while it can be deliciously enjoyable, worries me – I really don't want that method to *grow* and spread, weedlike, across even more of my personality. When I was younger I read with fascinated unease biographies of writers or actors or comedians (Peter Cook was one), who would so often say: there is no me, I'm only the performances. And I worry if, earlier still, when I was a kid, I just found that impersonations were *easier* as a way to get by. In primary school, in the playground, I used to do imitations of TV ads for cricket and other kids did quite like that. I imitated the high-pitched one that told us excitedly: 'The Pakistan tiger is coming!' Or the deeper tones of: 'It's on. The Benson and Hedges World Cup.' Kids would give me requests for other ads. I did Sunbeam Rice, for a while. I do seem to be saying more now, in this book, as plain me. Out from behind the act, putting my own face in the frame with a speech-balloon pointing to it saying 'oh my God!' I think this must come partly from wanting the relief of being known as me; from a need to say: this is the actual shape of my personality, distorted as it is, shameful, foolish, needy, incompetent, not-organised: here it is, here I am. And it is, I suppose, evidence of having more trust in people; talk openly as myself and I am saying: I reckon the rest of you will be kind enough to me even if *I*, not so protected, say this. The idea of that, the hope of it – that you could really tell more as yourself and survive – would be one of Garner's best gifts to me. That I'm even trying the amount I'm trying now is because of her. I begin to see that telling as yourself is a different way to get across Dad territory: you defy a suffocating authority by increasing the messages from only *one* self. I like that. I want some of that. Maybe. But let's look harder. I'm sometimes frightened of my method – its costs – but I'm still more frightened of hers. *She's* been frightened of it, she's said many times over the course of her writing life: I can't go on like this. In her *Diaries* Garner said she felt nothing but 'loathing' about her 'need to expose, thinly disguised or barely metamorphosed, my own experience'. And that 'What I do is bad and wrong. I'll have to learn some other way of writing.' But she also puts in, later: 'It was necessary for me to write this story.'

Garner did try, for a long time, to get out of the more direct method – the whole early-to-middle part of her writing life is her arguing with herself over whether she wanted to keep on telling so much as herself. In one interview, she said:

> I got pretty sick of myself in *Monkey Grip*.
> Not that I think it's bad, it's just when I look
> at it now I can see its self-indulgences, and I
> don't like very much the me that I see in that
> book ... It's been a great relief to get myself
> off centre stage.

What she really wanted, she says in that same interview, was to see if other 'technical advances' might be made. And what you can see, in her next three books, is Garner working, very fast and very well, at making those advances, at learning the more representational technique, exchanging the direct 'I' for telling as other people. But also finding, over these early-to-middle years, how much of her unusually strong and stubborn amount of 'I' could not be lessened, could not be made into anybody else.

In the first fiction she wrote after *Monkey Grip*, 'Honour', you can see Garner feeling her way, testing and adjusting the levels of seeing in and from *others*. Sometimes, I reckon it's fair to say, she gets the levels wrong, and overdoes how much can be known about another person. Halfway through 'Honour', two characters meet in the street and one is supposed to be able to *sense* this much of the other: 'flower, oil, coffee, soap: and under these, warmed flesh, dotted tongue, glass of eye, glossy membrane, rope of hair, nail roughly clipped'. But none of that over-ambitious perception matters as much as all the detail of others that Garner gets right, right away. There's a scene early on where Garner has to get the four people she needs for the next part of the story into a house, a room, say the wire on the door smells faintly of rust, say Kath is the ex-wife, Frank is the ex-husband but still Kath's good friend, and that they in their different ways are coping with Frank's new partner, Jenny. It's all exactly what *Monkey Grip* didn't have to do, kept in close as it was to just Nora. Now Garner gives us what can be seen when you display several others in motion: we're shown the little discomfitures and trying to be on their best behaviours that all three of these people are doing. And then Garner brings in, very deftly, the person who's going to make things even more difficult: Kath and Frank's kid, Flo, who really wants to show Kath Jenny's room, and all the nice things there. Garner adds: 'The two women stood awkwardly, embarrassed by the meaning of the bed.' And, from Flo, at Jenny's dressing table: 'See? They make your eyelashes *curly*.'

In *The Children's Bach*, the management of these not 'I's is done even better: there's no lingering in extra-perception to see if anything more can be found: instead, there's a new confidence, concision and pace; almost every sentence collects enough and then stops exactly where it should. So, at a kitchen table: 'The soup was thick. The bread was fresh. The stove's dry heat reddened their cheeks.' And you can see Garner move even more deftly in and out of the others she's made, taking a quick tour of the comedy, and sadness, of what's in all these different people's heads:

> The three women stood still and stared at one another.
>
> 'Sisters,' thought Athena, with that start of wonder which family resemblance provokes. 'Big one's tough. Little one's miserable.'
>
> 'She's beautiful,' thought Vicki. 'It's warm. I wish I could live here.' …
>
> 'She's a frump,' thought Elizabeth with

relief; but Athena stepped forward and held out her hand, and Elizabeth saw the cleverly mended sleeve of her jumper and was suddenly not so sure.

Later on, Garner does this jumping in and out even faster, makes it into a kind of roundelay; a quick sampling of good random amounts of others:

'Have you been to America, Philip?' said Vicki.

'The sort of singer who lounges across a glass piano,' said Elizabeth.

'I like to have tortellini of a Friday,' said Philip.

'She was wearing these daggy flares,' said Elizabeth, 'with embroidered insects.' …

'I walked in to our first gig,' said Philip, 'and they were sticking red cellophane over the lights. I thought, Oh *no*.' …

'They only cost twenty-five dollars,' said Vicki, 'so I bought two pairs.'

'Does anyone want more spaghetti?' said Athena.

And the life problem being worked on in 'Honour' and *The Children's Bach* is the same as the technical problem: how should you *include* other people? Who should you be with and stay with? In *Monkey Grip*, everyone was so young and not *bound*; Nora was poor, and lived in shabby share houses, and yes, was unhappy in love, but she could still spend so much time at the pool or the pub or dancing at a rock concert by the beach ('Oh,' she says, 'the looseness of the spine! and moving in the streaming salty air.'). They all could, Lou and Ange and everybody. Even someone as incapable and sickly as Javo still got to live in a kind of perpetual 'holiday'. None of the harder choosing had to be done yet. But in 'Honour' and *The Children's Bach,* Garner shows us people who are trying to figure out how much they should keep from youth – because it's too hard to stay as free, as loose, when you begin to understand you won't always have this youthful body, and you'll want to feel safer, more secure. In 'Honour', Frank stands in front of Kath, shows her the grey in his hair, and bursts out, 'I want a *real* place to live, with a backyard where I can plant vegies, and a couple of walls to paint, and a dog – not a bloody room in a sort of railway station!' In *The Children's Bach*, Dexter and his wife, Athena, have got this done, they have made a good home in Bunker Street, with a kitchen 'like a burrow' where the air 'shimmered with warmth'. But there is a kind of counter-pressure allowed for in the book: Dexter is so full of 'home', so in love with what he's made, with the victories of it ('Soup!' 'Soup means lots.') that he's left far too little for Athena. Oh, he says, 'Thena doesn't need that', she 'doesn't believe in make-up', all that muck, 'do you dear'. Marriage has made him so secure he's in danger of becoming a fool. Athena *is* longing to get out from her too snug, too tight home. And off she goes, to fuck Philip, the *guitarist*, who's sure not a family man: 'He paid … he spent money as fast as he got it', and who gives her plenty of attention, until, one morning, at the hotel, he 'neatly' takes 'his cock out of her' and begins 'to make some phone calls'. But Philip turns out to be, in his freedom, every bit as lost as Athena is: '"These last few mornings I've been shaving and I've looked in the mirror and thought, I could pull the razor across here like this" – he drew a line from ear to ear – "except that it would hurt so much."' And Dexter has never been cruel. He is generous (Soup means lots!). He just needed a lesson. So Athena does go back home. *The Children's Bach* ends with a burst of relief that you can go away from family, risk doing that, and still come back to it, find it all still there. In a bigger way, this has been part of what the book has been telling us all along; in its economy, its concision, the book has made a kind of promise, sentence to sentence, that it doesn't matter how much disorder there is, things can always be brought into order. Athena arrives at Bunker Street, having done what she needed to do and cleans all the mess away: 'She washed, she washed, she washed ... The sheets dried so quickly in the sunny back yard that before she had finished the cleaning she was able to remake the beds and tuck them in tightly.' A good home life – an orderly-enough *and* pleasurable-enough home life – is possible:

> ... and someone will put the kettle on ... and the tea will go purling into the cup ... the tables will be clean, the sun will be shining through the glass,
>
> and Athena will play Bach on the piano ... and her left hand will keep up the steady rocking beat, and her right hand will run the arpeggios, will send them flying, will toss handfuls of notes high into the sparkling air!

But then to read on, from *The Children's Bach* into Garner's next book, *Postcards from Surfers*, is to see – at least – two things: one, the technique gets even better. And two, the life-problems get harder and harder, nowhere near as cleanable. *Postcards* is Garner's first book of short stories, and in almost every one she keeps working so extraordinarily skilfully at finding out what's possible in the depiction of self and others. You get the feeling that, sometimes, even more than in *The Children's Bach*, she's relishing the staying outside of people, and the kind of brisk, impersonal efficiency she can find there: 'We heard he was back. We heard he was staying in a swanky hotel … We heard she was American. We washed our hair. We wore what we thought was appropriate.' That's at the very beginning of the story 'The Dark, The Light'. In other stories Garner will get back *in* closer to a more particular he or her: 'He played guitar. You could see him if you went to dance … at Hides or Bananas, horrible mandrax dives where no-one could steer a straight course … He supposed that there were questions which might be considered, and answered. He didn't try to find out. He just hung on.' ('Did He Pay?') Or in others, she'll make a consciousness more like what you would think of as her *me*, as Helen Garner's, but it's still held away, seen from more of a distance: 'It was a photo. She took it in her hand. It was herself. A small, dark face, an anxious look. And beneath the photo, under the glass, a torn scrap of paper … Her own handwriting said, *I'm sorry you had to sleep in my blood, but everything else I'm happy about.*' ('A Thousand Miles Away') She also makes this extraordinary variation of me, the me that's so distant it is almost like writing about someone else: me as a child. ('Little Helen's Sunday Afternoon') Garner is so good on the weirdness of being a child, the weird fact that you always seem shrunken, small in a world of the big, and the incongruous, estranging details of this; when her boy cousin carries her she sees, 'from her sideways and horizontal position', his 'big hip and thigh work[ing] under her waist like a horse's'. And she's also so good on the isolation, the fear, but also the primitive satisfactions, of being a child, the soon-to-be-forbidden enjoyments: 'Eating fast and furtively, bolting the food inside the big dark cupboard, she started to get that rude and secret feeling of wanting to do a shit. She crossed her legs and squeezed her bum shut, and went on guzzling.'

Through all these new variations Garner was still at work on the never-stopping problem of how much unruly, separate self should any little *or* big person keep? In *The Children's Bach* there was the hope of finding a quite happy compromise: freedom when you need it, and the chance to go back to the good, clean order of home. But in *Postcards*, it seems more likely you won't find enough freedom or enough order, you'll just get caught in a kind of painful wanting both: in the rip tides of both *please, me, I have to have me* and *please I can't stay out here, I'm too alone*. So many of the people in these stories have never learnt to do the necessary compromising, to give up enough individual-ness so they can really be 'together' with another person – and are beginning to suspect they never will.

'We'll have to start behaving like adults,' a lover says to an 'I', in 'Civilisation and Its Discontents'. And he adds: 'Any idea how it's done?' 'Well,' she says to him, 'it must be a matter of transformation. We have to turn what's happening now into something else.' But then they do talk about the kind of transformation they think they can get, exactly where they are, further from the usual 'home', where you can play, be different, 'bend the bars a little, just for a little … to let the bars dissolve?'

But this 'I' has already said that something else might be more important. She's told us that this lover she's with (who is married to someone else) 'had a way of holding me, when we lay down: he made small rocking movements, so small that I sometimes wondered if I was imagining them, if the comfort of being held were translating itself into an imaginary cradling'. This is not as excessive as wanting to be, as Nora did, 'absolutely enfolded'. But who doesn't want to be held? Who would want to get through life without someone to stay and hold you, who can be relied on to do this, and with it, give that most primal thing, that basic, basic message: I'm here too. It's not just you, you don't have to do everything by yourself. See how close I am? See how not alone you are?

In the stories after *Postcards*, 'My Hard Heart', 'The Psychological Effect of Wearing Stripes', and in *Cosmo Cosmolino* (which is made up of two stories, 'Recording Angel' and 'A Vigil', and a novella, 'Cosmo Cosmolino'), Garner keeps showing the consequences of too much separateness. Among these: if you stay too separate, even the closest people a separate person can have, your friends, might start to seem oppressively superior, people who just make you feel more alone.

In 'Recording Angel', the 'I' has a friend called Patrick, 'my *oldest*, my *most loyal friend*', who, from the comfort, the richness, of his own successful marriage, sits back and reminds her of how she saw him, years ago, on the street (when she was 'with some bloke or other') and that he saw her nearly call out to him, and then decide not to. And he says, 'luxuriously':

'It's rather like a Poe story, isn't it? … A person sees the chance of a better life passing by … makes as if to call out' – he flung forth one arm in the imploring gesture of a soul in torment … 'and then he slides down, and down, and down.'

I stared at Patrick, breathless.

'*Who* did?' I whispered. '*Who* slid down, and down, and down?'

He turned his full front to me … '*You* did, my dear! You!'

As many of Garner's separate people go on, into what they fear could be a down, and down, and down, it also becomes more obvious that this can happen to anyone, even those who *are* surrounded by all the plump cushioning of marriage, and family and home. Now, for the first time in Garner's writing, we're shown more and more deaths and suicides. We're told in 'Cosmo Cosmolino' that Chips died from a drug overdose, but a little girl at the funeral says he died '*by loneliness*'. Ursula, in 'Recording Angel' and 'Cosmo Cosmolino', dies from drink. Kim in 'A Vigil' dies from drugs as well – pills – but really more from a gradual failure to want to live in 'loneliness and fear'. Before Kim dies, she's frightened of the sound of children playing outside. Someone must be hurting them, she says. In 'My Hard Heart', a woman visits a friend whose husband is dying of a brain tumour. And the friend says:

> 'I used to think there was justice … and fairness. That there was a contract, that things meant something. Now I know your foot can

go straight through the floor.'

'And what's on the other side?'

'Nothing.'

'Nothing?'

'Nothing.'

At this point – if you, separate you, felt that you had 'fallen', and that even the more secure ones were falling too, if you were beginning to feel that, after youth, this is what *mostly happens* to people – you might very much hope that something could save you. To think about, to imagine, what could save you, what could be powerful enough to do that. In 'Recording Angel', the 'I' starts to get the sense that there might be something with her. Something that is following her, 'keeping pace with me wherever I walked'. And then she turns and sees it: at first she thinks it's a child – strangely – bent over and holding a gun. Then she realises what it is: 'He was a small, serious, stone-eyed, angel of mercy.'

This was a surprise for me, and I reckon for a lot of Garner's readers, this lump of the supernatural. Of a thing not of this world. And there's more of it, pretty soon. In 'Cosmo Cosmolino', Ray turns up at Janet's big, mostly empty house – or seemingly empty, for there is, all around, something else, something more. At first it appears only as its representatives, its messengers: the air, the wind, 'whispering', 'hissing', 'bumping' in the house; or a bird who always sings the same notes, 'over and over again', and comes and sits 'unblinking … virtuous' upon Ray's finger. Then *it* does appear, more as itself: Maxine, who also lives in the house, sees it. And Janet knows it's there: 'a lord', in the shape of a column, 'towering … featureless'.

Most of the rest of 'Cosmo Cosmolino' is about how these three – Janet, Ray and Maxine – try to cope with this *presence*, which is everywhere, sees everything, is 'manifest', 'vast', always so much more than any little human self. Janet – and this is important, the story does leave room for this – refuses it. She knows, she somehow *knows* that it wants 'some appalling and total submission ... a surrender of self with no hope of back-tracking'. And she fights it: 'with a mad pugnacious hubris she pitted herself; and at last a tremor rippled through the pillar, a slow, long shudder; and then it thinned, faded, and was gone'.

It's Maxine, who is very eccentric, who won't sleep in the house but insists she's better off in the shed, who builds her own furniture out of pieces of old wood and twigs; who often has very extravagant faith in things ('auras, star charts ... she believed that everything was meant') – Maxine is the one who's able to get the best of what this 'lord' has to give. She is, I think, part of an attempt by Garner to say: see, you can be this strongly individual – this unorthodox – and still be led by, blessed by, a higher authority. Maxine, one night, 'beyond reason', in a kind of trance, goes into Ray's room, holds *him* in a kind of trance, and becomes impregnated by him. And, through all this forgetting of what she usually is, and what is usually possible, Maxine finds she can create something so good, so unquestionably good, that it makes a new world, within this one:

> she would have it, out it would pop, and she would give birth to it, it would surge out all blind and bloody into the light, it would be born ... *Cosmo, Cosmolino*, world, little world.

And later, in even more of an excess of belief, Maxine finds she doesn't have to stay here, she can leave this world, this life, and go up, maybe join *it*, the presence, up there:

> What? ... Into her other sole pressed the iron pattern of the shed roof ... pop-eyed and dangling-breasted ... she looked down ... she ... stretched out, and thrust forth one arm as she had seen heroes and old-style swimmers do, the air smoothed into a bounding field of

congratulation … *Janet!* she yelled after them. *Your knickers! I've still got them on!* – but too late, too high – for *I* was over: *I* dropped off her like a split corset, there was no more *I*.

Maxine yelling about Janet's knickers is funny, but I do want to say carefully and respectfully that I think the rest is bad. And that I think almost all of *Cosmo Cosmolino*, all three stories in it, is bad. *Or*, as the rest of her work teaches me, I should try to say it more personally and admit: this 'religious' Garner is not the Garner I need; I need her to keep slogging away here, working away at the painful not-removable good amount of 'I' that has to be controlled and apportioned here, on earth. I don't want her to go up to where some magical other authority decides things; I am very unable to believe there is anything other than a human being who decides what a human self is, or can be.

But then I should say again: I've never risked as much of my more direct self as Garner, never worked so open, so exposed. I should show some humility about why Garner might have wanted to find out what the absolute *opposite of 'I'* could be. She made *Monkey Grip* very close to her own self, and then worked to imagine and depict the consciousness of other people. Then, from *Postcards* and the later stories to *Cosmo Cosmolino*, the process of finding and describing other people generated a kind of crisis of faith. Or a need for an excess of faith. All Garner's effort towards other people – the examination of even the best ways they could comfort each other – turned out not to be anywhere near enough comfort. Garner went from a persistent sense of separateness to an awareness that even those who are more attached to other people are still so frail, so vulnerable. That all human life, after youth is over, is a kind of waiting around for the worst things to start happening; whether you are alone or not, it doesn't matter: we are all booked for the sliding down, the fall, and then the nothing, extinction.

Your complete extinction. And if *this* is human life, this is intolerable and we have to imagine there is something else, something more than human, that can change it.

Of course, saying there should be a superior power doesn't necessarily make for bad art. The problem was that Garner's hope for some extraordinarily more powerful authority interfered with all her good selfish art instincts, the sense that *she* should make, *she* should choose more of the world. Big religious hope interfered with one of the most precious things she has, her special sense of aptness, of scale, in word-choosing. In *Cosmo Cosmolino* she keeps choosing bigger, fancier, 'important' words, words you'd need for all this bigger, fancier belief:

> Inside her, the little creature heaves for joy, her *Cosmo Cosmolino*, the errand on which she is speeding: can she endure this purpose? Is this what it has all been for? And does he hear

it too or is he secreting it, this wild interior music of gland and sinew, these grids of tough chords on which tremendous explosions leap and scamper, where nameless souls and sacraments outrageously disport themselves?

See that her accuracy has gone. Now we get the grids, the chords, on which explosions scamper. No they don't. They don't do that. And this new belief in some massive supervening authority also interferes with her storytelling. Parts of the story, details in the story, become improbable or not interesting because they're all proof of the same thing. The bird, the bird sings, the wind, the wind bumps, but – well. It's only you-know-who. This is the story-killing effect of exchanging a literary ordering principle for a religious one: in a religious story, everything is, in the most important way, already decided. Is under very superior orders. It is possible to introduce *some* religious logic into literature, many authors have:

Flannery O'Connor, *Dostoevsky* – even F. Scott Fitzgerald in *The Great Gatsby* has the giant eyes of 'Doctor T.J. Eckleburg' on an advertising billboard do some pretty heavy work as a symbol for the eyes of God (George Wilson, looking up at that billboard: 'You can't fool God!' 'God sees everything!'). But in our mostly secular society there's more prestige in doubt than in belief, and so religious meaning, if it's to survive in literature, I reckon has to be almost overwhelmed by a mass of *non*-meaningful detail. And you do see this in Dostoevsky, O'Connor, Fitzgerald, a crowding in of details that don't have to *be* anything else. And in *Cosmo Cosmolino* too many details are nothing but a substitute for the One Great Thing.

Plenty of people disagree with this dislike of *Cosmo Cosmolino*. Tim Winton, for one, is on record as saying he thinks it's Garner's best book, the book where she proved she would go 'her own way', become 'unreliable in the finest sense'. And that sort of praise makes me stop and wonder whether I should relax a bit, be more generous and say, C'mon, a writer should be allowed to experiment, to write a different book to the books they wrote before. But I mostly feel more dour, or pessimistic: I think that *Cosmo Cosmolino* was a real threat to Garner's whole career, that writers sometimes don't make it back from a *bad change*, that one's writing sensibility is thinner, harder to protect than a lot of people realise, that it can go wrong and stay wrong, that it's fair to say we wouldn't have Helen Garner, *the* Helen Garner, we have today if she'd kept making books like *Cosmo Cosmolino* – if we'd had three or four more books from this more elaborate, decorative, religious kind of writer. I can't help but think a big part of what makes her so extraordinary, of what guarantees her longevity, depends on what was written after *Cosmo Cosmolino*, and the very particular ways she was able to recover from that book and fight on, *here*.

After *Cosmo Cosmolino*, Garner did make another strong correction, even stronger than the one she made from *Monkey Grip* to 'Honour' and *The Children's Bach*. But this time, the move was not away from 'I' telling and into a more representational fiction. All fiction, representational or not, seemed to have trapped Garner, at least for a while, in something that made her feel too lost, and too hopeful for some extraordinary kind of rescue. So the strong move she made was to go to non-fiction, and find there, in this more public form, she could restore the more direct 'I' she ran in *Monkey Grip*, have *that* again, and not get to some point where she felt so alone or without order. She found a beautiful, risky, new combination: asserting again the more direct 'I' she always wanted, that she had her first faith in, but (and this is the crucial part and the great difference from *Monkey Grip*) now she took it *out-wards*, took all that unusual concentration of self and pushed it outwards, away from just lovers or friends and made it go talk to, be with, fight with, anybody, everybody. This is the hardworking secular settlement Garner made after *Cosmo Cosmolino*: there's no more of this 'the *I* dropped off'. Back down here she said: alright, I *do* want it, I do want a much more individual sensibility, but I can *only* have it if I really put it to work, really take it out, risk it, out in the world, this world, and see what *use* it is. Make it have an argument in public over how much self you should have, and how much authority over it there should and shouldn't be. This was the intense, sometimes aggressive, sometimes humble and uncertain work of Garner's first non-fiction book, *The First Stone*.

*The First Stone* starts with the transcript of an interrogation by detectives – a cold record of something pretty far away from any more-individual self: officialdom, group authority, literally *the police*. A man named Colin Shepherd states his full name and date of birth. And that he is the master, 'the chief executive officer' at Ormond College, a residential hall for students at the University of Melbourne. Then the detectives lead him through a series of questions about his behaviour at a college dinner-dance, and allegations from two students: one saying he touched both her breasts and her 'bottom', the other saying he cupped one of her breasts and squeezed it. Shepherd denies the allegations 'totally and emphatically'. He is told he may be charged with indecent assault. And the transcript ends with, 'Mr Shepherd, I am obliged to put some questions to you in relation to fingerprinting.'

Then, there's a swerve back *in* towards one self: suddenly, an 'I' is sitting at a break-fast table, reading a newspaper report about Shepherd's appearance before the Magistrates Court. And right away this non-fiction narrative includes so unusually much of this 'I''s immediate, not-thinking-things-through first emotion. The newspaper report is only about the second student's allegations; it doesn't even mention that more than one student said the master touched her in a sexual way. But this 'I''s first reaction is: 'He touched her breast and she went to the *cops*?' A little later on in the book, this 'I' will say: I don't understand what I'm feeling. I don't understand why I have so much first sympathy for the man in this story, and so little for the women. And: it could be because I was forced out of a job once for being – in a different way, but still – too sexual, for talking about sexual matters with my students. But at the breakfast table, when she reads that newspaper, there's none of this; she doesn't compare, or remember; she can't yet, she's feeling something stronger, she feels – not some milder distaste or dislike, but – 'horror'. 'Repeated rushes of horror'. The 'horror' coming, just as it did at the sight of that 'strangling' mat in the trees, from a heightened sense of *any* threat to the independence her self so desperately needs. That heightened sense, here, spills over into a kind of over-identification with him, an intense feeling that the threat-to-him is a threat-to-me. And she *has* to write to him:

Dear Dr Shepherd,

I read ... about your troubles and I'm writing to say how upset I am and how terribly sorry about what happened to you ... I expect I will never know what 'really happened', but I certainly know that if there was an incident, as alleged, this has been the most appallingly destructive, priggish and pitiless way of dealing with it.

So here we are: in a non-fiction narrative which includes this much fear, this much need, this much mistaken or *bad* reasoning. This much *attachment*. Includes exactly what almost all non-fiction excludes, is built on excluding, pretends doesn't exist. People do make essays and reporting that includes some kind of 'I' in it, but it's almost always a specially reduced one, the use of 'I' is only there to give a sort of limited verification: I was there, I was in the room, these things happened, I saw them. As the great non-fiction writer Janet Malcolm – who learnt this method herself at *The New Yorker* – put it, the 'I' is supposed to function with a more scientific detachment, more like 'the participant observer' in the 'fieldwork of anthropologists'.

Garner has said in interviews and speeches that when she was writing *The First Stone*, Janet Malcolm was the non-fiction writer she 'learnt from' and 'copied', the writer who really taught her how to 'dig her skates in'. And Malcolm, over the course of her writing life, did fight against this habit of pretending that you weren't at least in some way as confused and frightened and stupid as the poor subject. That you, stupid you, were also one of the 'natives'. Malcolm said, with some satisfaction:

When I first started doing long fact pieces, as they were called at *The New Yorker*, I modeled my 'I' on the stock, civilized, and humane figure that was *The New Yorker* 'I', but as I went along, I began to tinker with her and make changes in her personality … I gave her flaws and vanities and, perhaps most significantly, strong opinions.

So in her book *Psychoanalysis: The Impossible Profession*, as she reports on the analysts she meets and talks to, she also says, *I* was nervous, sometimes. And in *The Silent Woman*, her book about Sylvia Plath and the way people have attached to and against Plath, Malcolm goes further and says, Listen: the way I tell this story is going to be marked or changed by the fact that I identify with – I have more sympathy with – one of the people in it, a biographer of Plath, someone called Anne Stevenson, whom I never knew but admired from afar when I was an undergraduate. She was 'arty', Anne, she was a poet, and she always 'glowed with a special incandescence in my imagination'.

But what Garner does is more extreme and I'd say, in some way, more *truthful*. Which is not to slight Janet Malcolm; Malcolm can do things Garner couldn't do, isn't interested in; Garner would never, as Malcolm does in *Psychoanalysis: The Impossible Profession*, give you an outline of the entire history of Freud's thought, the fights he had with himself over how to organise it, and the ways people needed to organise it after his death; Malcolm will explain all that, give page after page of extraordinary elucidation of a complex intellectual system, and not as some dry exercise – Malcolm shows us why it matters, how people thought they could be helped by all this 'pattern matching'. But Malcolm is still, I reckon, too committed to *being intelligent*, removing too much of what is not intelligent away from her sense of self. Geoff Dyer has said that:

Reading Malcolm, I am often reminded of T.S. Eliot's remark that the only quality a critic needs is to be highly intelligent. The 'I' in her work is a kind of concentrate of learned, well-heeled cosmopolitan intelligence.

Garner shows the risks, but also the benefits, of not being 'intelligent' like that. Or, more: Garner makes a different argument about what intelligence really is. Malcolm will include that she was so anxious in front of those analysts, and that she saw the Plath story differently because in some way she wished she was Anne Stevenson. But she'll never let in as much of the untidy, the emotional, the bodily, more of the whole awful shameful human, as Garner does. It's hard to imagine Malcolm including, as Garner does in *The First Stone*, something as commonly untidy as blowing your nose. Or feeling a prickle on your neck. Or getting down on your knees, as Garner says she does, to try to pick up her bag from the floor. The entire point of being a certain kind of person, a cultivated person, an intelligent person, is that you *never* have to admit too much of that. You might be stuck in a body and a self, and be frustrated sometimes, unsuccessful, but never *very* unsuccessful. But this is Garner, halfway through *The First Stone*:

> I had to call Mr Donald E – to check two factual matters … Mr E – misunderstood my question and launched on an explanation of the wrong thing … Although his tone was only faintly irritated, I became flustered … Incredibly, though I was invisible to him on the end of a phone line, I even went on taking pointless notes … I actually *thanked* him and said goodbye. Then I sat here … flushed with astonished fury. I am fifty-one years old, and still at the slightest obstacle I regress into this ridiculous passivity.

Malcolm, very interestingly, reviewed *The First Stone* when it first came out. It's a peculiar review, with equal amounts of praise and disparagement. Malcolm said the book was valuable as a record of what people really feel, 'comparable to that of a patient in psychotherapy', and that's all – because if you present yourself as so 'unbalanced' a person, you can't be trusted to make a worthwhile assessment of anything.

But the unbalance is what makes Garner able to assess. Garner was effectively saying: my overreaction, my over-emotional letter to Shepherd, doesn't disqualify me, it qualifies me. Admit your overreactions, over-attachments, and you have a chance to see how shockingly much overreacting and over-attaching everyone else is doing. See more of the unfortunate truth about how psychologically extravagant, how 'heightened' we *all* are. Though – as in *Monkey Grip*, as with Nora – there is balance too, something to balance the excess, cool it enough, make it bearable. In *The First Stone* it is that the overreacting person telling the story is also trying to carefully and responsibly think about her overreaction, make a kind of special, detailed investigation of it – and working very hard to try to understand the overreactions of others.

So, soon after she's 'shot her mouth off' in that letter to Shepherd, Garner tries to talk to everyone, anyone, at the college, at the university, who might know something about what happened to the students, and what they think should be done about it. And what she finds, mostly, is that people have already formed into two great big hardened overreacting *groups*. One is a right-conservative group, which is for 'the college', Ormond, the institution, that grand old thing. This group is made up almost entirely of older men, men who lived at Ormond when they were students, thirty or even forty years ago (some are now members or former members of the college council), who don't feel that anything very bold, or disruptive, is needed, really, in a situation like this. The most important thing, one of them tells Garner, is to deal with Shepherd generously: 'You can't have a man feeling really sore and foul about the college.' Another old boy, now a judge, tells Garner, 'with a perplexed distaste', that there 'seemed to be a doctrine … that the family is inimical to the feminist cause, and that motherhood exploits women'. These are the kind of people who surrounded the students when they first made their complaint, and who, Garner finds, warned the students that their complaint may result in action against them for defamation. And who, after they conducted their investigation, expressed 'full confidence' in the master. It was only then, Garner says, that the students went to the police.

The other big overreacting group Garner finds is left-progressive, and this group is *for* the two students, this group is sure that Shepherd did what was alleged, and that his actions should be seen *only* as part of a much larger system of oppression. This group does see what it is doing as more like anthropology, science – something analytical. You do an analysis of who has power. Shepherd is a man. He was master of the college. Therefore: he had more power. That is really the only possible 'result', the only thing that can be *known*. One young left activist tells Garner it is this simple, because: 'sexual harassment is ultimately not *about* sex, it is about power'. And Garner, working much further away from any analytical or structural way of thinking, finds this exasperating: 'I don't see how you can unravel … two threads, sex and power, so neatly. They're tightly entangled. You can't *say* that – it doesn't *mean* anything.' Garner keeps saying that if Shepherd, as she puts it, 'forgot himself' at the dance, made a 'sleazy, cloddish' pass, let's not just 'analyse' this, let's, in a way, stay down with him; not think we are so much better or different or separate. She says, over and over: it can't be so simply and cleanly that he was 'power'. He may have done it because he had too little power, and was crass and sad enough to try for something he could never have. Garner says to the young left activist, 'As you get older you begin to understand that a lot of men in these harassment situations are *weak*. You realise that behind what you saw as force, there's actually a sort of terrible pathos.'

And of course people find all this effort against science-like thinking and politics-like thinking very irritating. (Whole books have been written against *The First Stone*.) *I* find it irritating. Or, more, worse: dismaying, upsetting. I don't want to stay down with Shepherd, sympathise with Shepherd or anyone like him, I want to stay up, with the good people, the left-progressive people who are seeing the *bigger structural problems* and doing the good work of fighting the bad old ideas about what can't change. I remember when *The First Stone* was published, I was twenty-four and at Melbourne University. When I read the book, the thing that hurt me the most was the disgusting idea that the left could make as many over-certainties and overreactions as the right. 'I noticed,' Garner says about another left-progressive person, that she regarded even asking questions 'as an attempt to intimidate her, and an instance of futile harassment'. So often, Garner comes across people on the left who say: we already know what this is. There are no questions needed, no arguments to be made. And even to *try* is an oppression. At twenty-four, having just got away from a world of many petulant conservative blokes, I didn't want to believe that We – the good, young we on the left – could be as caught, as stiff, as brittle, in our identification, our need, as my Uncle Terry. I wanted there to be one side that is the *good* side. But *The First Stone* says you never really get to have that. Try to stay too 'rigid' on any one side, in any of 'our carefully worked out *positions* and *lines*' and you'll only find 'the world is … scarier and more fluid and many-fold than we dare to think'.

But the risk of thinking like that is that you'll never help make enough of a *necessary* new 'position' or 'line'. You'll never see enough of what is so necessary and courageous in joining together and making an effective campaign to stop something. One of *the* other reasons I think *The First Stone* irritates or dismays or upsets people is because it works so hard to recognise the human-ness of Colin Shepherd, to make you see that, yes, we don't know for certain what happened at that dinner-dance, and yes, he lost his job, and yes, he'll never be able to do the work he could do ever again, and yes, his life has been ruined, and yes, possibly he was punished out of all proportion to what he'd allegedly done, yes, yes; but the 'I' in this book doesn't seem to do enough to say: those students were part of making a really needed new rule, that we could and should have, which is: that the master never gets to touch her tits. Ever. Those young students made it more likely that women could go through their whole education and work-ing life without any man 'forgetting' himself. And putting that hand there. They worked and got us a little closer to a rule, a standard, that would make it as unlikely, as career-ending, to touch her breasts, as taking a piss on the office carpet. Those students did what should have been done, to get to a little more civilisation.

Except that Garner does say this. Reading and rereading *The First Stone*, I often found that I'd have an objection to it, blame it for not saying something, and then see that it did say it. So Garner does say that those students had the courage 'to confront … the whole apparatus of power in its panoply'. And she includes the idea that if Shepherd was punished too much, maybe it *has* to be this way, maybe someone has to be made an example of, 'or they'll go on getting away with it for *ever*.' But I reckon another risk of including your own overreaction is that we, the readers, will tend to remember the hottest, messiest overreactions (Garner: when those students wouldn't talk to me, 'I wanted to … shake them till their *teeth rattled*') and not the more beneficent, humble work done afterwards (Garner: I thought about how hard it must have been for the students to do what they did, I thought their 'determination' so 'impressive', and I do sometimes think that they were right).

And that risk is there again in Garner's next book, *Joe Cinque's Consolation*, where her first overreaction is so blatant that all the work done against it is, maybe, much harder to remember. It *is* such a risky method, including so much psychical excess. But it shows something that thousands – millions – of primly reasonable 'reports' or 'discussion papers' never show: how much primal emotion really is inside us, and how much harm can come from not even admitting it exists. *Joe Cinque's Consolation* shows what a very non-emotional administrative system can do to some people who get trapped in its workings: two older Italian immigrants, Maria and Nino Cinque, whose son, Joe, was killed by his mentally ill girlfriend, Anu Singh. Singh, in the midst of various paranoid fantasies about her need to die and to take Joe with her ('We were supposed to go together!'), laced his coffee with Rohypnol and, while he was passed out, injected him with heroin. And Garner packs the first part of the book with her hotly excessive identification with, and reaction against, the 'narcissistic' Singh: 'With dread I recognised her … the figure of what a woman most fears in herself – the damaged infant, vain, frantic, destructive, out of control.' But, again, Garner does extraordinary work to think through how much control, or punishment, of a bad self should be allowed:

> Every morning for the next two years, I sat down to read the papers with the scissors in my hand. Nothing interested me but murder, trial, punishment. I hunted out accounts of psychiatric expert evidence. I compared different judges' styles of sentencing, trying to perceive the reasoning behind them … I read trashy tabloids that railed against

the leniency of courts, screamed for harsher sentences, trumpeted about what it cost the taxpayer to keep murderers in custody. I collected horrors, pointlessly, fanatically, in a sort of secret grief.

And, again, Garner sees the overreactions around her – this time, the ones that are even harder to see, the ones that call themselves 'the judicial process'. Garner sees how preoccupied the court system is with correctly classifying Singh, with measuring her level of illness, using techniques such as the 'Minnesota Multiphasic Personality Inventory'. And all the time, the Cinques sit there in court, having to watch this, and trying in their not-so-educated way to make the court recognise more that their son is *dead*, their son has been *killed*. Nino says, later: 'My son haven't done nothing wrong. My son was innocent. Let them kill the son of the judge, the barrister. Then they understand.' And Garner keeps saying it too, says here he is, see, in the photographs of the crime scene, a 'trickle of black muck running from one corner' of his mouth: 'This is Joe Cinque. Joe Cinque is dead.'

The historian and essayist Inga Clendinnen took a very high tone against this kind of thing, telling a group of lawyers that *Joe Cinque's Consolation* 'exemplifies what you ... are up against. It exemplifies the layperson's way of "doing justice" ... Garner's "heart-felt" narrative is utterly impatient of the slow business of due process and the cautious accretions of common law.' But this is to miss what Garner's narrative is really doing: Garner is not trying to replace the working of the law (she says clearly that the court's, the judge's, 'reason' and 'detachment' are necessary, are 'hard-won' and 'dearly paid for') but to give it a vital interruption, restore what any administrative system will probably never include enough of, because it is too hard to measure, to *systematise*. Clendinnen should have tried to think and feel more for the

Cinques, who didn't fit so easily into the Minnesota Multiphasic Personality Inventory. Garner, admitting her emotion – saw their emotion. Saw that when the evidence described Joe as 'gasping for breath', Maria Cinque 'lurched forward and clutched her arms to her belly, as if she had been stabbed'. Garner wanted to show that something like this was *as important* as anything else under discussion in that trial.

The irritating idea for Clendinnen, I suspect, was that an amateur could see something the professionals couldn't. Garner is, in *Joe Cinque's Consolation* (and *The First Stone*), a kind of extraordinary amateur – one who works as hard as any professional, but never loses her amateur sensibility, asking the questions that have been 'accreted' away: 'Where does all the woundedness, the hatred *go*? What becomes of the desire for vengeance, for a settling of the score?' Are these so 'emotional' we can't include any of them in how we make our law? As she asks these kinds of questions,

Garner gets at the way, as Charles Taylor puts it, 'the bureaucratic mode of life ... splits reason from sense'. The way that, when we try to cope in public with something that is so sad and grievous, we make it into smaller, more manageable units. Into an 'inventory'.

But then Garner worked on to find the place where this isn't done, or is done the least. To find where the most *good* administration is possible. I think that's what is being carefully examined and reconstructed in *This House of Grief*, Garner's book on the trial and conviction of Robert Farquharson. 'Robbie' Farquharson was a 'hard-working bloke', a cleaner from Winchelsea, a little dumpy 'teddy bear' of a man, who did nothing exceptional his whole life – divorced, 'a discarded husband' but, still, ordinary enough – until he drove his car into a dam and murdered his three kids. Three little boys: aged ten, seven and two. Jai, Tyler and Bailey.

The 'I' in *This House of Grief* who'll tell us about what happened – tell us about Farquharson, the night the boys died, and all the work in the courts that came after – will still include plenty of her smaller local untidiness. She'll say she stumbles around cooking and 'keeps dropping things', or that she 'feels her heart go boom' when one of the barristers tells her off for talking about one of the trials in public. But this time, there isn't any first identification. There's no fear that something that is *me* is being taken away, or needs to be fought for. There is, instead, a sense of *us*. The 'I' still gets to turn up, so to speak, but now it says: I'm here not so much for me, but for *us*. (I'm a 'citizen', she says, 'a curious citizen'.) And part of an *us* that can work to do something about Farquharson. With the healing sense that an order is possible, a little like there was back in *The Children's Bach*, but now taken further, now working to order something so much worse, some of the worst possible private disorder, worst possible self-ness. A self that did something so horrific because of some wrong it thought it had suffered. Because it wanted to punish his ex-wife. (A family friend testifies at the trials that Farquharson said of her, when he saw her with her new partner, 'Nobody does that to me and gets away with it … [I'll] pay her back big-time.') And punish his children ('I hate them'). And when the Major Collision officers come to Farquharson in hospital and say, you understand the boys didn't make it out of the dam, he says, 'So what's the likely scenario for me?' And again: 'I mean, what sort of thing's going to happen to *me*, now?'

But Garner shows that all around Farquharson, all around what's he's done, there are people asking fair questions, doing good work. This time, we get an interrogation that is part of this good work. Garner pays the closest attention to the video of Farquharson's first interview by the homicide detectives. Farquharson says he *coughed*, he had a coughing fit, he coughed so much he *blacked out*, and that's why he drove into the dam. It was so *dark*, it all happened so quick. He tried to get the boys out, he tried. And the detective, Clanchy, 'takes his chin out of his palm' and says, 'How *did* he try, though?' And later, in court, the prosecutor, Tinney, asks: 'You could have leaned over and undone the seatbelt on Bailey?' And almost at the same time that Farquharson sits up in hospital and asks, What'll happen to me now? a police diver named Rebecca Caskey gets into the dam. And the 'I' telling is interested in nothing so much as seeing what Caskey did; this ordinary but extraordinary work:

The water was black and very cold. She could not see at all … She started feeling bits of metal and plastic … Then she bumped into something with her head, something that moved. She touched it with her hand. It spun freely. A wheel. On the witness stand she squeezed her eyes shut, put her long-fingered hands out in front of her, and mimed blind groping gestures up and down an imaginary wall. 'What was facing me,' she said, 'was the underside of the car. It was vertical.' … 'And then,' she said, 'I felt, slightly protruding from the car, a small person's head.'

And this 'I' stays and watches interview after interview, witness after witness, stays with it, for years. Farquharson killed his sons in September 2005. He's first tried in August 2007, and found guilty. But that verdict is set aside, because of a procedural mistake by the police, in December 2009. Then he's tried again in May 2010. In October 2010, he's found guilty, again, and sentenced to a minimum term of thirty-three years in jail. He appeals, and is rejected, in 2012. Then he appeals again, this time to the High Court, in 2013. And then, at last, there's no more. All the work is done. The work of enough of us is done. And the 'I' who has followed all this is able to say: look what we can do. *This House of Grief* is a hard-worked-for argument about the extension of our self, our care to others – how much we can feel and do for someone not me, not mine:

> When I let myself think of Jai, Tyler and Bailey lying in their quiet cemetery … I imagine the possessive rage of their families: 'You never knew them. You never even saw them. How dare you talk about your 'grief'?
>
> But no other word will do. Every stranger grieves for them. Every stranger's heart is broken. The children's fate is our legitimate concern. They are ours to mourn. They belong to all of us now.

This is a strange thing to say about a book about a man who murdered his children – but *This House of Grief* is hopeful. It has a kind of tough, proven optimism in it, because it shows we, as a group, can judge properly. It's hard work, but we can do it. What was so wanted in *Cosmo Cosmolino* – powerful good authority – can be made, here.

And Garner celebrates it:

> When the tipstaff called us to our feet and ceremoniously opened proceedings – 'All persons having business before this honourable court are commanded to give their attendance, and they shall be heard' – I had to bite my lip to keep from shouting, 'Amen!'

Now, I'm a little shy about this. I feel – not the dismay I get when I have to fight with *The First Stone*, but something milder – a discomfort. A smaller niggly amount of: *no, not that much,* at Garner's feeling that the courts can do *so* much good. I think of the O.J. Simpson trial or the trial of Rebekah Brooks (from *The Sun*, in England, tried for phone hacking, defended well – expensively well – and walking free). And I wonder too, little sourer me, less loving-the-group me, whether if I'd been in that courtroom I'd have been so impressed by, say, prosecutor Tinney, who might have seemed, in all his good work, pedantic, finicky, cold; not some universal friend. Garner does allow that the defence counsel, Morrissey, is 'perhaps a little vain'. But, again, I'll try to take a correction from Garner, and say my sourer sense (my against-Them sense) can't see enough of what courts, even in our society, our capitalism, do get done; that they *are* the places where, for example, Donald Trump couldn't keep saying he won that election. Courts are – still, enough – as Garner says in her *Diaries*, places where '*They really do have to prove it*'. And, given what we are, given the rest of what we do, that is something worth saying an amen to.

And it's not as if Garner is just for the rules and the institutions now. *This House of Grief* is her strongest statement of how fine the work of a group can be, when it judges and punishes an individual. But she never gives up the ambition to run extra and near-illegal amounts of self. What Garner ends up with is: an acceptance of group order that is also always saying: yes, and I'll make my *own* order. This is from the essay 'The Insults of Age', which is a kind of fighting manifesto of how much Garner is going to decide for herself, at seventy-one:

A friend and I were strolling along Swanston Street ... Ahead of us in the crowd we [saw] a trio of ... lanky white Australian school-girls ... One of the girls kept dropping behind her companions to dash about in the moving crowd ... [I saw the girl] with a manic gri-mace thrust her face right into [an] older woman's ... The girl skipped nimbly across the stream of people and bounded towards her next mark, a woman sitting on a bench ... Asian, also alone and minding her own busi-ness. The schoolgirl stopped in front of her and did a little dance of derision, flapping both hands in mocking parody of greeting ... In two strides I was behind ... I reached up, seized her ponytail at the roots and gave it a sharp downward yank. Her head snapped back. In a voice I didn't recognise I snarled, 'Give it a rest, darling.' ...

Now my blood was up ... The world bristled with opportunities for a woman in her seventies to take a stand. I shouted on planes. I fought for my place in queues ... I wouldn't say I was on a hair trigger. I was just primed for action.

I say amen to that as well.

After a long fight for more self and less self, it seems to me Garner did get to a beautiful, strong kind of *both*. She was able to keep something wilder, more aggressive, less conformist, *and* make herself into someone who could work for years to see what the group is doing, respect what the group is doing. It's so rare to develop both of those sensibilities so acutely. Much more often, people with a strong individual sense just stay further away, and send the rest of us reports from their refined or anxious or angry separateness. (And they should. Again, given what we are, given all our cruelty and stupidity, I reckon it's defensible for some people to say: *I'm staying out*, or even *I'm staying out and I hate you all*. Like Swift, in *Gulliver's Travels*, saying human beings are nothing but Yahoos.) And then, as often, people with a strong group sense, over time, just *merge* their self more and more into the group. (Philip Roth, in his book *Patrimony*, wrote that whenever his father got into difficulties, he would tell stories about the family, and the extended family, about all the difficulties they had, 'on and on' so he was 'no longer someone alone', but always 'a member of a clan, whose trials he knew and accepted, and had no choice but to share'.) But there is also a third possibility: me-apart-and-with-the-group. A separate self that is always working against its separation. A separate self that respects what a group can do, but is, because of its separateness, very watchful for what a group gets wrong. That is suspended, always, between *I want to be out* and *I want to be in*.

I think Garner's dearest hope was to be, committedly, intensely, *out and in*. To find there an honourable settlement. Find there that the thing that made all your unsocial noticing possible – your first separation from family – could turn out to be unexpectedly *useful*, useful to exactly the people you felt so separate from. And, in this in-between-ness, find that the people you felt so separate from are useful to *you*. In 'Postcards from Surfers' it is shown that the father – along with all his bad over-deciding – could still kindly teach his child. The 'I' in that story remembers being a little girl, walking by the wharves with him and him saying gently enough, 'See that rope? It's not a rope. It's a hawser.' And him saying, a little later, 'Listen … listen to the wind in the wires.'

When he was old, Garner's father came to live next door to her, she invited him to. He began to actually ask his daughters for advice. 'In the car,' Garner wrote in one essay, 'we were always laughing.' And the day he died, when he was having trouble breathing and the ambulance came to take him, Garner knelt down and strapped his sandals on. What you can get to, *out-and-in*, is the good ambiguous truce of: I'll never be like you, but I don't have to hate you. What you can get to is: They hurt me, but maybe not as much as I thought they did. And I can help Them, maybe more than I thought.

Garner helps me to see that, I can try to follow her to there. That a more separate self could be kept, and somehow be brought back towards Them, is my dearest hope as well. I want it partly because Garner makes me think and remember and compare and realise my They weren't *that* bad. And I have to give up the luxury, the complacency of thinking they were. In all their why-is-the-boy-doin'-that, stop-the-boy-doin'-all-that-reading, let's-kill-the-boy's-personality, they still fed the boy, clothed the boy, put a band-aid on the boy if the boy fell down. I would never say anyone *has* to come back towards Them. But I think I can, I should. Because some of my separation hasn't been examined enough, hasn't been *earned*. Has been – an overreaction. Or, at least: I should never stop working to see what could be an overreaction. I do have my own memories of something like 'hawser', and 'listen to the wind in the wires'. I'll always be grateful to Garner because she helps me be more truthful about father, and family, and home, when it would have been so easy – *I* would have found it so easy – to keep on being resentfully, angrily inaccurate. For years.

And when I started this book, I thought my job was to go on learning from Garner, go on into her method, into her less disguised telling. I thought I should try as much of that method as possible, because I was sometimes frightened of the way I'd used disguises to keep me separate, and that Garner's method was the antidote. I said I wasn't going to try to 'transfer' into her method, that would be such an obvious mistake, such an obvious wish to be taken away from what I'm mostly going to have to do. But I reckon that's *exactly* what I was wishing for. I reckon that wish has always been lurking in my feeling of affinity to Garner. It's my version of a *Cosmo Cosmolino*–like extravagant wanting to be changed, saved, taken *up* and away to somewhere else. I can't believe that the mighty changing force could be a god, but I'll believe it could be another writer, a wonderful writer. But can I come back down now, to some more realistic sense of what I could actually learn from Garner. Which is, I think: that there might not be any antidote. And – this is so important – you'll sometimes really *wish there was one.* Wish you weren't stuck with the problems and the shame of one particular method.

Garner fought to keep telling less socially agreed things as herself, but she also tried very hard to get out of that method; said she felt so much doubt and shame and 'loathing' about it. Then, equally, I can read Zadie Smith saying she's long felt 'self-loathing' because she *does* use disguises. But Smith also says she can beat back the shame of what can seem so abnormal, so dishonest:

I was struck by an old cartoon I came across somewhere. It depicted Charles Dickens, the image of contentment, surrounded by all his characters come to life. I found that image comforting. Dickens didn't look worried or ashamed. Didn't appear to suspect he might be schizophrenic or in some other way pathological. He had a name for his condition: novelist.

The lesson seems to be that you'll very likely be ashamed of *any* method you use to try to tell less social things. Maybe because any attempt at being less social almost inevitably invites self-hatred. Tell more, disguised or not, and you'll set off what Adam Phillips, in his essay 'Against Self Criticism', calls the 'obscene severities of conscience': that part of you – your mind, your self – that will persistently, repetitively, try to stop you daring to say what we don't usually say. In different kinds of writing, here comes the same self-loathing. And *wishing* there was another way.

I can make some effortful progress away from

my usual I'll-say-it-pretending-to-be-others method. I can tell you openly it was *me* – or a lot of me – on the trundle bed, not knowing how to have an orgasm. But I notice, when I told you that as myself, I was always a little more formal, a little more reserved, than when I told it in character. I didn't get to 'Oh my god!' telling as me, I don't think I'd ever get to something as loose, as unguarded, as accurately incompetent as 'Oh my god!' I *chided* Janet Malcolm for taking so long to include more of her real personal disorder, and said isn't it a shame she couldn't go further, but me, little me, if *I* have to talk as me, *I'll* still cling to as much 'being intelligent' as I can, so I'm not like all the fellas and footy blokes I grew up with. As me, just me, I don't want give up the clever controls. And I notice too that in this whole book I haven't given you one specific incident, telling as me, about my family, my dad, my mum. About Mr and Mrs O'Beirne. I can't, I can't give them to you. But 'Mr and Mrs O'Dingle' – I'll tell you what *those* people did. As soon as I make some new names, as soon as I get the freedom of some substitution, it is remarkable, I get a feeling in my head like all the lights coming on, my own lit-up feeling of *permission*.

So maybe I can say, happily enough from my place in the junior writing division: I tried the more open method, I tried to look hard at it, but I think I might be *set* much more on one side, and one side only. Garner was able to swap over, for a while, and put on some disguises, and then found she had to arrange her writing around her more direct self – *that* was her surer permission, her surer way to telling less socially accepted things and being able to withstand it. Impersonation could be the price I always have to pay. I may have laboured to arrive back fairly close to where I started – but I suspect it's often like that. You have to do so much work, sometimes, to see the most obvious thing about yourself. If I *am* stuck mostly in impersonation, I do have more of a feeling now that all the risk might still be worth it. Even the risk of being made sick by too much impersonation could still be worth it. It could be worth it for the *more* I can get: more telling against Them, more coming back to Them. I'd still take the amount I could get, hoping it would save me more than it harms me. It would still be – without sounding too highfalutin about it – the best way I can live.

But may Garner's influence keep working on me! May it always work on me! Let me keep inching towards even a little of what she does. If an antidote is too much to hope for, let me keep trying for a vital supplement. That could be enough. No wish for 'total' change, just an expectation that I can try for some correction, while not being too ashamed of a method that *does* bring me so much freedom. Let me be happy enough with what I maybe mostly have to do, while also being continuously drawn to her example. And I wonder, in the end, if that's true of almost all of us?

Almost all her readers? Almost all of us watching what she does from a lot more cover. Taking what we can from her, or trying to. And, hopefully, not making any mistake about how good and strange and rare she really is.

# NOTES

3–4    'In an essay just called "I" … "filled me with horror"':
Garner, 'I', *Meanjin*, Volume 61, Number 1,
January 2002, pp. 40–43, also available at
https://meanjin.com.au/essays/i/

Many writers and critics have said that the need to
make literature comes from an unusually strong dislike
of feeling part of a group. Richard Rorty talks about
the literary writer's desperate need to 'find distinctive
words or forms', and to stay near whatever is, in some
way, 'exhibiting a discontinuity', in *Contingency, Irony,
and Solidarity* (Cambridge University Press, New York,
1989, pp. 24, 25). Harold Bloom uses the same word
as Garner: 'horror', the literary writer feels 'a horror' of
becoming 'only a replica or a copy' (Harold Bloom, *The
Anxiety of Influence*, 2nd ed., Oxford University Press,
New York, 1997 [first published 1973], p. 80).

    You could, I suppose, feel that 'horror' and still want
to reform the group – but the specifically literary sensibility is one which refuses even that much dilution of
the self into any general *plan*. The literary sensibility
shies away from anything too general – abstractions,
concepts, structures – anything which it perceives as not

close enough to the self. This is what I mean by '*closeness to self*' and 'the more individual self': it's a very particular need for separation from groups of other people *and* from groups of thought. The literary writer is almost helplessly drawn, over and over, to feelings and observations that can't be easily grouped into any big 'system'. Drawn, over and over, to what can't be assimilated, to the continuous unorthodoxy of detail.

Garner has *such* a strong amount of this literary sensibility. In one interview she said she works 'from that part of yourself which is not amenable to organisation or routine or even conscious control' (Kate Grenville and Sue Woolfe, *Making Stories: How Ten Australian Novels Were Written*, Allen & Unwin, Sydney, 1993, p. 62). And in her *Diaries*, she talks about reading Peter Handke and feeling 'intense pleasure at the tininess of his observations. Actually, they're not so much moments as junctions between moments. When I read them I feel that I am not after all crazy or even weird. I feel strengthened, *private*, encouraged. I feel the worth of very small things' (Garner, *Yellow Notebook: Diaries Volume I 1978–1987*, Text Publishing, Melbourne, 2019, p. 123).

Later, she has to fight hard against the influence of her third husband, named only as 'V'. 'V' is another writer, and he wants to have a more literary sensibility, to be an unorthodox noticer, but, Garner says, he 'is always talking about *symmetry*' (*One Day I'll Remember This: Diaries Volume II 1987–1995*, Text Publishing, Melbourne,

2020, p. 19). 'V' is often taken aback by Garner's continuous literary noticing: 'He reads me a lovely piece of Goethe's conversations with Eckermann. "He must have cleaned that up a bit when he wrote it down," I say … He stares at me in silence, even more shocked than he was when I said that a certain pink iced bun at Bondi looked like a Fairweather' (*One Day*, p. 77). Sometimes Garner longs to be more like 'V', 'intellectual, contained' (*One Day*, p. 3). But more often, she's quite sure of her strength: 'Everything that can be called A SUBJECT he knows about. And I know about the rest' (*One Day*, p. 24).

5    'hard rail of will': Garner, 'The Psychological Effect of Wearing Stripes', first published in *Scripsi*, Volume 5, Number 1, June 1988, p. 104, republished in *Stories: The Collected Short Fiction*, Text Publishing, Melbourne, 2017, p. 167.

7    'Garner calls all of that "clonking" certainty': Garner, *True Stories: Selected Non-Fiction*, Text Publishing, Melbourne, 1996, p. 170.

13   'An interviewer once asked Garner, "You talked about how people have one story in them"': Gina Mercer, 'Exercising the Muscle of Curiosity: A Conversation with Helen Garner', *LiNQ* (*Literature in North Queensland*), Volume 24, Number 2, October 1997, pp. 28–29.

14   '"My father," Garner wrote in her *Diaries*, "is incapable of conversation"': Garner, *Yellow Notebook*, pp. 157–58.

15    'Erving Goffman wrote that': Erving Goffman,
      *The Presentation of Self in Everyday Life*, Penguin,
      Harmondsworth, 1969 [first published 1959],
      pp. 20–21.

30    "I hated it … I'm painted as this self-destructive
      fool, really': Liz Burke (producer) and Fiona Tuomy
      (director), *Helen Garner's* Monkey Grip, ABC TV,
      2014. The man who was 'Javo' did change his mind,
      though, about *Monkey Grip*. After saying for years he
      hated the book, he eventually told Garner, 'now I love
      it. My only criticism of it is that you should have left
      in all our real names': Garner, 'I', p. 40.

32–33 'Karl Ove Knausgaard asks exactly this in his book
      *My Struggle*': See Knausgaard saying why he doesn't
      use fiction disguises – and fighting with himself
      about whether he should – especially in these parts of
      *My Struggle*: *My Struggle, Volume 2: A Man in Love*,
      Harvill Secker, London, 2013, pp. 630–31, and *My
      Struggle, Volume 6: The End*, Harvill Secker, London,
      2018, pp. 176–81, 826–27, 972–79 and 1007–11.

33    'inhuman': Knausgaard, *My Struggle, Volume 6:
      The End*, p. 989.

39    'In his book *The Anxiety of Influence*': Bloom, *The
      Anxiety of Influence*, Preface, p. xxx. Bloom is in
      particular talking about the difficulty some writers
      have coping with Shakespeare's extraordinary 'freedom
      of representation'.

40    'Montaigne saying: "I am loath even to have thoughts

which I cannot publish"': Michel de Montaigne,
'On Some Lines of Virgil', in *The Complete Essays*,
trans. M.A. Screech, (revised ed.), Penguin, London,
2003 [first published 1595], p. 953.

40    'Knausgaard saying that he didn't masturbate until he
was nineteen, and then telling, as no-one but himself,
how he did manage to get that job done': Knausgaard,
*My Struggle, Volume 5: Some Rain Must Fall*, Harvill
Secker, London, 2015, pp. 96–98.

40    'Sheila Heti, in *Motherhood*, saying: my partner Miles
wanted to put his cock': Sheila Heti, *Motherhood*,
Henry Holt, New York, 2018, p. 215.

41    'Instead the words *I love you* come tumbling out of my
mouth in an incantation the first time you fuck me
in the ass': Maggie Nelson, *The Argonauts*, Graywolf
Press, Minneapolis, 2016, p. 1.

*The Argonauts* is a beautifully made argument that you
can have explicit reporting of a personal life *and com-
bine that* with more abstract, systemic thought. Nelson
combines close descriptions of her individual life with
ideas and quotations from Wittgenstein, Gilles Deleuze,
Judith Butler, Eve Kosofsky Sedgwick, and others. But
I'd still argue that Garner's refusal to include any idea or
quotation from any more tightly organised intellectual
system – any theory, any metaphysics – has its own
value. That Garner's strong discontinuity, her refusal
to systematise her thought, has a special power to help

us see idiosyncrasies, exceptions, details, that even the best theory might prevent us from seeing. And I'd argue that you don't have to choose between these two sensibilities: the most desirable thing would be lots of people reading Maggie Nelson *and* Helen Garner; reading strong writers informed by theory, and strong writers not informed by theory. Instead of – which so often happens – people mostly reading only one kind of writer and not the other.

44     'George Eliot called it "the extension of sympathies"': George Eliot (Mary Ann Evans), 'The Natural History of German Life', quoted in Rosemary Ashton, *George Eliot: A Life*, Hamish Hamilton, Harmondsworth, 1996, p. 156.

44     'Arundhati Roy's phrase for it is "softening the borders"': Arundhati Roy, 'The Language of Literature', in *Azadi: Freedom. Fascism. Fiction*, Penguin, London, 2020, p. 90.

46     'it is what Garner, in her *Diaries*, calls "Dad territory"': Garner, *Yellow Notebook*, p. 198.

48–49 'In her *Diaries* … nothing but "loathing" about her "need to expose, thinly disguised or barely metamorphosed, my own experience"': Garner, *Yellow Notebook*, p. 9. '"What I do is bad and wrong. I'll have to learn some other way of writing" … "necessary for me to write this story"': Garner, *One Day*, pp. 51, 225.

50 'In one interview, she said: "I got pretty sick of myself in *Monkey Grip*"': Kevin Brophy, Myron Lysenko and Nolan Tyrrell, 'Interview: Helen Garner', *Going Down Swinging*, Number 7, Autumn 1986, available at: https://goingdownswinging.org.au/2016/archives-interview-with-helen-garner-1986/

74 'The book where she proved she would go "her own way", become "unreliable in the finest sense"': Tim Winton, quoted in Bernadette Brennan, *A Writing Life: Helen Garner and Her Work*, Text Publishing, Melbourne, 2017, p. 120. For more detailed arguments in favour of *Cosmo Cosmolino*, you could start with Kerryn Goldsworthy, *Helen Garner* (Australian Writers Series), Oxford University Press, Melbourne, 1996, pp. 1–5, 59–63; and Tegan Bennett Daylight, 'Consider This: Helen Garner's *Cosmo Cosmolino*', *Sydney Review of Books*, 13 May 2016, available at https://sydneyreviewofbooks.com/essay/consider-helen-garner-cosmo-cosmolino/. And you'll find more examples in the notes to Goldsworthy's book and to Brennan's *A Writing Life*.

81 '"the participant observer" in the "fieldwork of anthropologists"': Janet Malcolm, *The Journalist and the Murderer*, Alfred A. Knopf, New York, 1990, p. 161.

81 'Janet Malcolm was the non-fiction writer she "learnt from", and "copied", the writer who really taught her how to "dig her skates in"': All these quotes are from Garner's speech at the 'NonfictioNow Conference' held

at RMIT, Melbourne, November 2012; no transcript seems to be available, but you can see the full speech at https://www.youtube.com/watch?v=8rfsXsBg3IU, or hear it at www.wheelercentre.com/broadcasts/nonfictionow-melbourne-2012-an-evening-with-helen-garner. See also Garner's introduction to the Australian edition of Malcolm's *Forty-one False Starts: Essays on Artists and Writers*, Text Publishing, Melbourne, 2013, pp. ix–xi.

82 'When I first started doing long fact pieces': Katie Roiphe, 'The Art of Nonfiction Number 4: Janet Malcolm', in *The Paris Review*, Number 196 (Spring 2011), pp. 126–151, p. 134.

83 'Glowed with a special incandescence in my imagination': Janet Malcolm, *The Silent Woman: Sylvia Plath and Ted Hughes*, Alfred A. Knopf, New York, 1993, p. 13.

83 'Malcolm shows us why it matters, how people thought they could be helped by all this "pattern matching"': See Malcolm on the beauty, and distortions, of Freud's intellectual system in *Psychoanalysis: The Impossible Profession*, Alfred A. Knopf, New York, 1981, pp. 6–47; and in her essay 'Six Roses *ou Cirrhose?*' in Janet Malcolm, *The Purloined Clinic: Selected Writings*, Alfred A. Knopf, New York, 1992, pp. 31–47. The phrase 'pattern match' is in the 'Six Roses' essay, p. 39.

83–84 '"Reading Malcolm, I am often reminded of T.S. Eliot's remark that the only quality a critic needs is to be highly intelligent'": Geoff Dyer, 'The Absent Woman: Janet Malcolm', in *Anglo-English Attitudes: Essays, Reviews and Misadventures 1984–1999*, Abacus, London, 1999, p. 267.

86    'Malcolm, very interestingly, reviewed *The First Stone* when it first came out': Janet Malcolm, 'Women at War', *The New Yorker*, 7 July 1997, pp. 73–75; republished in Janet Malcolm, *Nobody's Looking at You: Essays*, Farrar, Straus and Giroux, New York, 2019, pp. 230–37. Garner didn't mind the review: 'Even her disagreements don't sting, because she writes as if *I* had written almost unconsciously ... (Also, she used the expression "this extraordinary book")': Garner, *How to End a Story: Diaries Volume III 1995–1998*, p. 110.

90    'Whole books have been written against *The First Stone*': See a complete list in Brennan's *A Writing Life*, p. 166. The most important, I reckon, are *Bodyjamming: Sexual Harassment, Feminism and Public Life*, Jenna Mead (ed.), Vintage, Sydney, 1997, which has a contribution from one of the students who made the complaints, and Virginia Trioli's *Generation F: Sex, Power and the Young Feminist*, Minerva, Melbourne, 1996, republished with a new forward and afterword as *Generation F: Why We Still Struggle with Sex and Power* (Scribner, Sydney, 2019). Trioli argues strongly against Garner's use of 'the idiosyncratic, personal approach' (p. 34) at pp. 33–42.

97  'The historian and essayist Inga Clendinnen took a very high tone against this kind of thing, telling a group of lawyers': Inga Clendinnen, 'Making Stories, Telling Tales: Life, Literature, Law', 18th Lionel Murphy Memorial Lecture, 17 November 2004, quoted in Brennan, *A Writing Life*, p. 227.

99  'As Charles Taylor puts it, "the bureaucratic mode of life … splits reason from sense"': Charles Taylor, *Sources of the Self: The Making of Modern Identity*, Harvard University Press, Cambridge, Massachusetts, 1989, p. 500.

106  'Courts are – still, enough – as Garner says in her *Diaries*, places where "*They really do have to prove it*"': Garner, *Yellow Notebook*, p. 183.

110  'Philip Roth, in his book *Patrimony* … his father … "no longer someone alone", but always "a member of a clan"': Philip Roth, *Patrimony*, Simon & Schuster, New York, 1991, p. 71.

114  'Zadie Smith saying she's long felt "self-loathing"': Zadie Smith, 'Fascinated to Presume: In Defense of Fiction', *New York Review of Books*, Volume LXVI, Number 16, 24 October 2019, available at: https://www.nybooks.com/articles/2019/10/24/ zadie-smith-in-defense-of-fiction

114–5  '"I was struck by an old cartoon I came across somewhere"': ibid.

115  'What Adam Phillips, in his essay "Against Self-Criticism", calls the "obscene severities of conscience"':

Adam Phillips, 'Against Self-Criticism', *London Review of Books*, Volume 37, Number 5, 5 March 2015, available at: https://www.lrb.co.uk/the-paper/v37/n05/adam-phillips/against-self-criticism; republished in *Unforbidden Pleasures*, Hamish Hamilton, London, 2015, pp. 84–121, p. 92.

# NOTE ON FURTHER READING

This book has been only about one part of Garner's writing – the strength and rarity of her fiction and non-fiction techniques, and the kind of questions and pressures these put *at* me, another, more junior writer. I'm very conscious that a lot of what is interesting about Garner has been left out, so please do go to Kerryn Goldsworthy's book *Helen Garner* (Australian Writers Series), Oxford University Press, Melbourne, 1996. It'll give you more of what Goldsworthy calls the 'cultural and historical context' (p. 7) of Garner's writing, and a much closer view of the arguments it set off in the media and in the universities. Goldsworthy pays particular attention to the way Garner's work became part of some of the most difficult arguments ('faultlines' and 'dilemmas') in feminist theory (p. 6). Published as it was in 1996, *Helen Garner* only discusses Garner's writing up to the essay collection *True Stories: Selected Non-Fiction*, but it's especially valuable nonetheless as an overview and assessment of what Garner was, and *was taken to be*, in the first half of her writing life.

The other book to go to is Bernadette Brennan's *A Writing Life: Helen Garner and Her Work*, Text Publishing, Melbourne, 2017. I've already cited it a couple of times in the notes: it's the most comprehensive book available about Garner's life and writing. Brennan recorded dozens of interviews with Garner's friends and the people Garner worked with, and was able to see all of Garner's not yet released papers in the National Library in Canberra. *A Writing Life* is full of detailed biographical and literary information about *all* Garner's books – including ones I haven't even discussed, such as the early novella 'Other People's Children' and the screenplays *The Last Days of Chez Nous* and *Two Friends*. And Brennan's source notes will be your good guide to finding pretty much everything else written and said about Helen Garner's work.

# BOOKS BY HELEN GARNER

### FICTION

*Monkey Grip* (1977)

*Honour & Other People's Children* (1980)

*The Children's Bach* (1984)

*Postcards from Surfers* (1985)

*Cosmo Cosmolino* (1992)

*My Hard Heart: Selected Fiction* (1998)

*The Spare Room* (2008)

*Stories: The Collected Short Fiction* (2017)

### NON-FICTION

*The First Stone* (1995)

*True Stories: Selected Non-Fiction* (1996)

*The Feel of Steel* (2001)

*Joe Cinque's Consolation* (2004)

*This House of Grief: The Story of a Murder Trial* (2014)

*Everywhere I Look* (2016)

*True Stories: The Collected Short Non-Fiction* (2017)

## SCREENPLAYS

*Two Friends* (1986)

*The Last Days of Chez Nous* (1992)

## DIARIES

*Yellow Notebook: Diaries Volume I 1978–1987* (2019)

*One Day I'll Remember This: Diaries Volume II
1987–1995* (2020)

*How To End a Story: Diaries Volume III 1995–1998*
(2021)